Taveira Sports Architecture

Taveira Sports Architecture

INTRODUCTION BY MEL GOODING · ESSAYS BY EDWIN HEATHCOTE AND MAGGIE TOY

ARTMEDIAPRESS

Contents

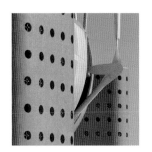

Published in Great Britain in 2004 by **ARTMEDIA PRESS**
Culvert House, Culvert Road, London SW11 5AP

ISBN: 1 902889 11 8

Printed and bound in Italy

Tomás Taveira: Fields of Dreams

Tomás Taveira is an architect of poetic vision and resourceful invention. Few architects of world standing have so exuberantly exploited the new possibilities of form and colour that became available to architecture in the last third of the twentieth century. Behind his characteristic use of brilliant polychrome surfaces, of strong pattern and contrast, and his tendency to structural agglomeration – to the powerfully expressive juxtaposition of bulging block, tower and column, corner and curve, right angle and diagonal – is a deeply informed architectural imagination. His architecture responds to a triple imperative: the first is that of a total *visual* environment, of which pre-existing buildings form a vital part, and which must have physical integrity, beauty and dignity; the second is that of effective social use and multiplicity of purpose; the third is that of formal individuation, by which the building achieves distinctiveness and clarity of presence. For Taveira, each aspect is conceived within the ambit of the pleasure principle.

His CAD projections, such as the virtuoso series created for the Albufeira marine complex, are definitively postmodern *fantasias*. But their cumulative multicoloured clusters or attenuated sequences of irregular forms, like everything that Taveira creates, have an intellectual and moral provenance in the idealism of classical Modernism, while their eclectic stylistics at the level of feature and detail are an effective critique of the puritan aesthetic whose economy determined the austere high-modernist identity of form and function. They may be seen, indeed, as a late-century response to, among many other things, Malevich's pure white 'arkhitektons', those wood and plaster dreams of a future architecture of pure cubic volumes, to the orthodox orthogonals and primaries of De Stijl, and to the harsh and colourless concrete

Mel Gooding

severities of international post-war Brutalism.

Taveira is a practical idealist. To be practical is to take proper account of all human requirements, including the need for environmental variety, surprise and delight. Taveira's Postmodernism was never a matter of idiosyncratic decorative caprice, but a freely constructive imagining of humane *utility*. He was thus uniquely predisposed, it seems, to become the pre-eminent contemporary architect of places whose purposes are primarily recreational. His resourceful use of the cool and elegant engineering we associate with High Tech, especially in the football stadia presented in this volume, has not inhibited his palette of festival colours or his repertoire of exhilarating organic-geometric forms. He has determined to create structures and spaces that will intensify and enhance the already heightened spirit of those who come to watch the beautiful game.

Taveira approaches the design of the stadium as one who is himself excited by sporting spectacle. As a football fan (and ex-player) himself he knows the pride and passion of partisanship, and he has a profound awareness of the ritualised release of emotional energies that makes the modern football match (and other sporting occasions to a lesser extent) central to cultural definitions in our time. He knows also of the many diverse demands now made upon sporting complexes as places of pleasure and business, and of their function as the potential focal point of regenerative urban development. Taveira's stadia, with their astonishing structures and thrilling canopies framing the arena of play, served by superb satellite facilities, are total theatres of social action. They are in themselves spectacular events.

Sports Architecture

The history of stadia building has been dominated by engineers rather than architects. In fact it is only in relatively recent times that architects have become involved. This may seem remarkable as the stadium is one of the city's pivotal communal buildings, a venue for shared emotion and release and a setting where the particular locale becomes tremendously important. More than any other type of building, the stadium and the crowd which fills it, is a building about its own location, a home for the home fans, possessing a powerful spiritual connection to place and community.

From the Colosseum in Rome to the Maracana in Brazil, the stadium has always been about release, fundamentally about keeping the working classes entertained and diverted. The Romans were fully aware of the dangers of the mob; the brutal games enacted within the Colosseum were notoriously a way of sating the mob's bloodlust. The thronging crowds who cram into the Maracana are escaping their broken-down *favelas* for a few hours of communal well-being and unfettered partying. We do not know who the architects were for either stadium yet they are among the most famous buildings in the world. Partly because of its status as the place of release of the most dangerous elements, stadium architecture has been associated with something necessary but unwholesome. In *The City in History* Lewis Mumford writes: 'The arena and the bath were, in fact, the new Roman contribution to the urban heritage, one contaminating it, the other purifying it: both conceived as colossal structures for mass entertainment, at a time when mass organisation demanded spatial compactness and high density of occupation. These two forms came into existence together and vanished together.'

Both the arena and the bath house reappeared at the dawn of the modern age across Europe. The stadium at least spread across the world quickly, one of the key new building types of the twentieth century. When the sporting arena was resurrected it was only as a pale shadow of its Roman predecessor but it was just a matter of time before the architectural possibilities of the stadium as icon were realised again.

Perhaps architects have finally spotted this potential: the stadium as a shop window for their talent, taste and practical planning skills; or perhaps it is to do with the increasing bourgeoisification of sport – contemporary, well-heeled crowds will not put up with the pseudo-medieval conditions endured by their fathers' generation. Perhaps it is partly to do with the increasingly sophisticated services required, and certainly it has something to do with the stringent building regulations that have arrived in the wake of crowd tragedies in

Edwin Heathcote

stadia across the world. Whatever the reason, in recent years architects from some of the most innovative international offices have come to dominate stadia design. Twenty years ago it would have been impossible to imagine the demolition of London's Wembley Stadium and its famous twin towers, let alone the building of its high-tech replacement by Norman Foster. It would have been impossible to imagine practices of the intellectual calibre of Herzog de Meuron, Cruz & Ortiz, Fumihiko Maki and Eduardo Souto de Moura getting involved in stadium design. These practices worked on art galleries, classy houses for the metropolitan elite; maybe, occasionally, innovative social housing. Not football stadia. Now each new international tournament brings forth a host of worthwhile, often fascinating new buildings by world-renowned names.

This is an important advance not just for architecture but for urbanism and planning. From the time of the Romans, the stadium was a pivotal urban building, a semi-public space that played a critical role in the lives of the citizens. Its central urban location reflected its importance to metropolitan life, as did its detailing, decoration and ambition of scale. In the nineteenth century, it had been supplanted in its pivotal urban role by the buildings of bourgeois culture: the opera house, the theatre, the museum, the gallery, the library, the university. These civic palaces became the buildings expressing a city's pride in its physical structure. Although often grand, sports buildings from the nineteenth century were practical as opposed to interesting architecture. As mass sport, particularly football, became more firmly established as working-class entertainment, the stadia became increasingly marginalised, from an urban and from an architectural point of view. They were pushed to the urban edges, positioned in cracks behind railway junctions, beside factories and sidings, adjacent to major highways or tucked away in obscure suburban side-streets. The cities grew around these sites, leaving them in a paradoxical position – both central and yet marginalised. Football grounds had been made accessible to their working-class audiences by their proximity to railways. Crowds were dependent on trains for transport to away games. With the spread of the car, a momentous change occurred and stadia were moved once more to the peripheries, dissociated from their power base of local fans, positioned deep in the wastelands that surround contemporary cities. Football stadia moved out to the suburbs and, in a few notorious cases, the defection of a team led to a collapse in the sense of place. When the Dodgers left Brooklyn, blue-collar New York lost a big part of its identity. It was a seminal

Dr. Magalhães Pessoa
Municipal Stadium, Leiria

moment in the life of the city (Brooklyn writer Paul Auster writes eloquently about the pervading and persistent sense of loss), one which has been repeated on a smaller scale in less iconic cities across the globe. The stadia lost their importance as urban markers, as extensions of the public space of the city and became sterile vessels, only populated once a week by crowds who had travelled great distances to be there. This was a phenomenon equally true of the baseball and football stadia of the USA and of the soccer stadia of Europe and Latin America.

This divorce of the sporting stadium from its inner-city location had profound and disastrous consequences for sports architecture. The buildings became stand-alone objects, big roofs unrelated to their surroundings, not anchored in their communities, either physically or aesthetically. The last thirty years have seen the return of stadia back to city centres, now often replete with derelict sites of the post-industrial landscape, made more attractive by government and international grants for regeneration programmes.

Both in Europe and the USA major strides have been, and are being made towards the reintroduction of architecture into the sports world. For the 1992 Olympics Barcelona reclaimed land from the old docks of the city. In the same year, Camden Yards in Baltimore saw the reintroduction of baseball (Washington DC's local team, the Baltimore Orioles) to the centre of a ravaged city, also dominated by its docks and naval tradition. The stadium has been used as a tool of regeneration, and sport has helped to knit damaged communities and urban fabrics back together. The Portuguese stadia of Tomás Taveira are firmly rooted in this new tradition.

Potential in Portugal

For some countries major international football tournaments have been used to foster or rekindle the passion of a people for the sport. Thus we have seen a World Cup in the USA, another in Japan and Korea and a startlingly successful venture in France, a country that had famously lost its enthusiasm for the game but dramatically found it once more with the incentive of home soil (and a supremely talented and attractive team). Portugal is a different case entirely.

There are few places in the world where passion for the game is as intense, where love of team and the game influences both political and financial decisions and where sectarianism among supporters is rife. It is a Latin phenomenon (although not exclusively), a trait shared with Italy and Spain where football is life, a tenacious extension of civic pride and

Dr. Magalhães Pessoa
Municipal Stadium, Leiria

local solidarity. It is also a culture that has fostered some of the world's finest teams and most extravagantly skilful players, even if the national team has often underperformed.

Thus the purpose of stadia architecture in Portugal, in football at least, is twofold. Firstly to inspire the confidence and pride in the supporters and the teams themselves, and secondly to use the buildings to revitalise parts of cities which, by European standards, remain poor. Taveira, with his José Alvalade Stadium and buildings at Leiria and Aveiro has the task of reinvigorating the teams and the cities. He is doing this with an extraordinary blend of inventive engineering, dazzling colour and complex geometry. Taveira is a populist, a populist with a profound love of football. He even played for Benfica as an adolescent, although he tells me he was 'a highly poor player' going almost immediately to play for a smaller team for a couple of seasons until his studies got in the way. Whilst it is tremendously refreshing to see avant-garde offices from Herzog de Meuron to Souto de Moura engaging with the architecture of mass sport, it seems wholly natural to see Taveira, who has been designing flamboyant sports buildings for much of his career, constructing some of the country's most important stadia.

Alessandro Mendini, the Italian designer and pioneer of Postmodernism, wrote of Taveira that he was 'an established architect of a great bourgeois metropolis, able to impose a strong image on his city with large-scale interventions'. Indeed, his interventions into his home city of Lisbon are spectacularly visible. From the mega Postmodernism of his Amoreiras complex (1980–86) and the monumental bank HQ for BNU (1983–89) to the garish underground interior of the Olaias metro station (1998), Taveira has made a significant if controversial impact on the usually restrained city of Lisbon.

Portuguese architecture is known internationally for a group of architects renowned for their subtlety and for their self-effacing, minimal oeuvre. Chief among these is Alvaro Siza, possibly the most universally admired modernist working in Europe today. The work of Siza's master Fernando Tavora, and of Eduardo Souto de Moura, is tremendously well respected internationally, indeed the latter is designing the stadium at Braga, a building partly hewn from the rock of a local quarry and one of the venues designated for the Euro 2004 football tournament. Through these architects Portugal has gained an international reputation as the home of a certain kind of subtle critical regionalism. Taveira is not a part of this group. Categorically. Taveira's work is an extraordinary magpie blend of elements drawn from anything from De Stijl

Dr. Magalhães Pessoa
Municipal Stadium, Leiria

canvases to Frank O. Gehry's dancing constructions, from the garish colours of childrens' toys and postmodern ceramics to the populism of streamlining and Miami Art Deco.

If Siza, Tavora, Souto de Moura and others draw on the simple, unselfconscious, blocky monochrome forms of the Portuguese and broader Mediterranean vernacular, Taveira's work seems more informed by the sensual excesses of the Portuguese Baroque. Indeed, if one considers the function of the church as the centre of a community, as the venue in which that community comes together to become one as a congregation and collectively to experience a communal ecstasy, then that analogy becomes quite apposite for the stadium. The brilliant colours and sculptural forms, the bulging stair towers and structural pylons as spires and campanile, the mosaics and the undulating roofs seem to refer directly to that ecclesiastical architectural tradition. Taveira's work is easily identifiable as part of a Latin tradition, a tradition which embraces architects who are not afraid to experiment in structure, decoration, colour and undulating, organic form. It is a tradition embracing Antonio Gaudí in Spain, Eladio Dieste in Uruguay, Felix Candela in Mexico and Ricardo Bofill in France, as well as countless others. In his work on stadia, Taveira draws on other seemingly disparate sources.

In terms of structure his designs draw on the British high tech tradition, with a recognisable vocabulary of brightly coloured pylons and complex roofs. There is the more sophisticated, elegant engineering tradition of the Italians, in particular the works of Pier Luigi Nervi and his successors, notably Renzo Piano. Very apparently, there are the sculptural, free-form experiments of Frank Gehry, the sometimes dancing, sometimes crumpled or collapsing volumes which have made Gehry the most famous and in-demand architect in the world.

What made Gehry a superstar was his design for the Guggenheim Museum of Art in Bilbao. He became famous partly for his remarkable architecture: for new forms made possible by computers and aerospace technology, architecture which seemed to grow out of its surroundings (the Bilbao docks) like a freak vegetable nurtured on steel and reflective water. More importantly, Gehry is a superstar for what his building did for Bilbao.

The gallery dramatically transformed a city that had suffered greatly from the decline of its industry and its port. Almost overnight a single building, a building defined, significantly, more by its architecture than by its contents had turned a provincial industrial backwater into an international destination, a magnet for so many tourists, weekenders and

Dr. Magalhães Pessoa
Municipal Stadium, Leiria

day trippers. Gehry's building completely redefined international civic attitudes to architecture, demonstrating its ability to draw crowds and how a single structure can spark a city-wide regeneration. This remarkable transformation of Bilbao with his art gallery and, more recently, neglected downtown Los Angeles with his Disney Concert Hall, has prompted many of Gehry's contemporaries to attempt to do the same with far less exclusive structures, stadia.

Portugal, a former imperial power and once one of the wealthiest of all the world's nations, has seemingly been in decline for centuries. Although beautiful, it is not a country of spectacular landmarks and its cities are short of internationally recognisable icons. The capital, Lisbon, was stripped of its oldest structures by the devastating earthquake of 1755 and it remains low on the towers and domes which help to define the world's tourist centres. The Euro 2004 tournament is a fine opportunity to reinforce the international image of the country with new, impressive sports structures.

Stadium Architecture

Stadium architecture has been through several recognisable phases, each generally marked by a single, epoch-defining structure which changes the way architects, engineers, the public and the professionals think about the venue. The scale, ambition and coherence of the Maracana in Rio de Janeiro (begun 1947) inspired a generation of stadia across Europe and the Stalinist Eastern bloc. The Houston Astrodome in 1965, and its spiritual brothers the Tokyo Dome and the Toronto Skydome a couple of decades later, ushered in an era of multifunctional stadia able to accommodate numerous sports and rock concerts, in all weathers. This type of structure proved particularly influential in North America where a blend of extreme weather conditions and audiences used to air conditioning triggered the need for covered stadia – a staple building type. In Europe, with its focus towards football alone as a mass-market spectacle and its temperate climate, there was a tendency to favour open-air structures. The structure, however, which exerted the greatest individual effect was not a football stadium but a structure built to house the Olympics in Munich.

The Olympiastadion (1965–72) was designed by engineer Frei Otto and architect Günter Behnisch in one of the most successful and complete collaborations in the history of sports architecture. Behnisch and Otto's brilliant structure heralded a new age of High Tech, introducing an architecture that could mimic the undulations of artificially constructed

Dr. Magalhães Pessoa
Municipal Stadium, Leiria

landscape and expressing the tensions and forces acting on the dramatic, sculptural roof. It was a return to the engineering traditions from which sports architecture had emerged, but also a move towards using the structure to generate the architecture, and the two became inseparable. What is so brilliant about the Olympiastadion is that the undulating roof and the pylons which support it are all there is. The structure is its own architectural expression – questions of style disappeared. It is almost impossible to exaggerate the effect, both direct and indirect, of Behnisch and Otto's structure. Indeed, the effects are still being powerfully felt, from the elegant profile of Macary, Zublena, Regembal and Constantini's Stade de France to HOK-LOBB's Millennium Stadium Cardiff.

The looming influence of the Olympiastadion is visible in the expressive, expansive roofs and the spiky pylons which dominate contemporary stadia design. It is there, if obliquely, in the work of Tomás Taveira too. In Taveira's architecture the curvaceous roofs are always tempered, or perhaps anchored, by a blend of urban rationalism and gaudy, colourful, post-modern exuberance. While Frei Otto's work and that of his disciples appears as a free-flowing sculptural object, a trait particularly noticeable in the Olympiastadion, Taveira has always tried to root his buildings in an urban context, even if

that context may be imagined and even if it involves a caricatured accumulation of objects. The striking cover of a recent Taveira monograph consists of a montage of brilliantly coloured architectural forms, bits of existing and proposed structures from housing and urban interventions to stadia. It is an apposite image for his architecture which can rely on exactly that kind of bold and often seemingly jarring juxtaposition.

This approach is very clearly demonstrated in the designs for the Faro/Loulé Intermunicipal Stadium. In Faro the undulating roof is surrounded by a series of brilliantly coloured forms looking like stacked toys. It is seemingly a strange move as both roof and terrace structure form a coherent whole. It seems odd then to attempt to break up or dilute that coherence with such a sequence of often random-looking objects. What this does, however, is to begin to key a huge, imposing structure, which will inevitably be dead most days of the week and times of the day, into the scale and active life of the city. In fact where there is no city, just a scruffy brown field development that so often surrounds stadia, the attempt is made to generate a mini-urban context.

A self-generating urban approach is even more visible at the Dr. Magalhães Pessoa Municipal Stadium in Leiria. Here there is a similarly sensuous roof structure and embracing,

Dr. Magalhães Pessoa
Municipal Stadium, Leiria

wrap-around curtain wall, with the pylons puncturing the membrane roof. An agglomeration of elements surrounds the structure and supports it (acting as pods containing service elements and access routes). The effect is as if a town had begun to grow around the stadium, an encouragement, a demonstration of how the first delicate steps of urban regeneration could be taken. These elements introduce the scale of the surrounding environment, whether actual or imagined. It is an unusual and virtually unique methodology. Other designers have introduced geometric elements to temper single, monolithic forms. Service and access elements added to existing buildings retrospectively are the most obvious examples of these, Milan's San Siro Stadium being a well-known case with its bulwark-like access ramps contained within those distinctive stripy cylinders. Yet no other architects have adopted this oddly hybrid approach. It is a thread which has run through the work of Taveira since the 1980s and his huge buildings are often knitted into the urban fabric with these devices. In the early 1990s Taveira began to adopt free-form shapes as well as geometric and platonic solids. It is these irregular blocks that have dominated his work in recent years. Crumpling, undulating volumes can be seen in the designs for Aveiro and Leiria and evoke the spectre of Frank Gehry's 'Dancing Buildings', more particularly his Fred and Ginger Building in Prague where twin towers wrap around corners and each other in an extraordinary, kinetic display. They also bring to mind the Bilbao Guggenheim, Jørn Utzon's Sydney Opera House and Gehry's Disney Concert Hall in downtown Los Angeles, all key structures which reinvigorated architecture and the public building as icons for the city

Spanning the globe, these buildings accommodate high culture, art, music and opera. Thus, no matter how hard the architects try to make them synonymous with the cityscape, they are often destined to remain arts ghettos. Taveira is introducing the most populist ideas drawn from the oeuvres of these architects to bring contemporary architectural culture to the masses, to huge, genuinely international and socially mixed audiences on the terraces.

Portugal and Football

Football appeared early in Portugal, courtesy of the English whose influence was still powerfully felt during a century of close political and trading cooperation. Surprisingly, it wasn't until the beginning of the twentieth century that the game began to really take off with the official formation of clubs. Portugal's football association, the Federação Portuguesa de

15

Sports Architecture

Futebol was founded in 1914. The country's first international engagement was a friendly against neighbours Spain in 1921. The Portuguese lost 3–1 in a match played in Madrid, sparking one of Europe's historic sporting rivalries. That Spain was the front-runner in the bidding to host the Euro 2004 football tournament and was beaten by the Portuguese bid proved a sweet revenge. Portugal was a founder member of FIFA in 1954 and in the following decade the national team began to make a memorable and indelible mark on the international scene. Mozambique-born Eusébio proved one of the finest players the game has known and, one of a 'golden generation' of international players in the 1960s, led club side Benfica to the UEFA Championships in 1961 and 1962. The national team went through another golden phase in the 1980s but Portugal gained a reputation as the nearly nation, with a team of consistently high-class players who delighted with their skill and grace but never seemed to fulfil their potential. Partly because of a persistent lack of success in the international field, Portugal, a country of 10 million, has never before hosted a major international sports tournament so it was a surprise choice to host the European championship. But in terms of both football and culture, Portugal punches above its weight.

In contemporary football, Luis Figo is regularly cited among the top three or four players, perhaps as revered as Eusébio was in his day. His proclamations are listened to with huge interest, his word can be enough to make or break a politician and, while his move from Barcelona to Madrid caused a virtual revolution in Spanish football, he remains a god in a native country that has come to terms with his desertion of the national game. The game has an entirely different status in Portugal than in say, England, France or Germany. While the passion exists in these countries, footballers remain at best fashion and TV celebrities. In Portugal they are seen as universal men. Although the almighty Figo is gone, there remains plenty to celebrate in Portugal. Benfica, Sporting Lisbon and FC Porto have been consistent fixtures in the international club scene, their successive teams always delighting and impressing. The official tag line of Portugal's Euro 2004 bid was simply 'We love football'. It was a blend of naivety and truthfulness.

Culturally, and particularly architecturally, Portugal is in a fascinating and influential position. The architectural and design scene is vibrant and genuinely diverse. The approaches of Souto de Moura at his stadium in Braga, a minimal structure partly hewn from the rock of an abandoned quarry, and

Dr. Magalhães Pessoa
Municipal Stadium, Leiria

Taveira with his riotous, brilliantly coloured structures could not be more different. The tournament has brought together new stadia from architects as diverse as these, and from international firms including HOK; they have built a unique and important set of sports structures, the effect of which will be felt long after the last match has finished – not just in terms of their design and innovation, but in their impact on the cities and communities into which they have been inserted.

What is attractive about Portuguese football is also attractive about its architecture. Both sport and design are exercised with a passion that can lead to intense emotion. Just as the rivalry between the Lisbon clubs, Sporting and Benfica and FC Porto in the north can seem extraordinarily bitter, on a scale matched in Europe only by that between perhaps Real Madrid and Barcelona or Celtic and Rangers, architects too engage in ferocious rivalry and internecine disputes.

This creates the most stimulating background for the phenomenal injection of adrenalin this tournament will give Portuguese football. Euro 2004 is to be held in eight cities extending from Braga and Guimaraes in the north to the coastal region of the Algarve in the south. Of the ten stadia approved for the games by UEFA, half are completely new structures, and the others have been extensively revamped to meet current standards. The legacy these stadia leave cannot be overestimated. As well as national pride and the reinforcement, and also resurrection, of traditional local loyalties, they effectively become the physical fabric of the future of Portuguese football and of the nation's sport as a whole.

Sporting Architecture: Community, City, Building

The text so far has been largely concerned with the architecture of football and undoubtedly it is the sport that has defined European stadium architecture. Football generates spirit and arouses passion like no other game, but this can mean that its venues become adored despite, as much as because of, the success of their design. Early football stadia were ugly but functional, designed to afford the most basic seating and occasionally shelter the crowd of working-class supporters. Ticket prices have risen and corporate interests have begun to dominate the game.

Clubs have responded by commissioning finer buildings to accommodate corporate interests and their VIP guests, and the increasingly middle-class and well-to-do supporters. The commodification of the game's top players and the gradual transformation of supporters from fans into consumers have left both football and its fans in the twenty-first century in a

very different position compared to twenty-five years ago. Although wealthier clubs have become dislocated from their fan bases, socially divorced from the industrial working classes who were, and usually remain, their lifeblood, communities still require facilities for participatory sport. It is in the spirit of local teams and contests that the community is able to regain its direct influence over sport in the wake of corporatisation in professional sport.

These community sports buildings are far more concerned with the everyday life of the city, being used every day of the year. Integrated into the urban fabric, these structures have the ability to become indoor plazas, real architectural equivalents of public space. It is exactly with such buildings that Taveira has experienced great success in recent years, enlivening often drab town centres with a series of strikingly colourful and vividly playful structures.

All Taveira's sports and community structures adopt a micro-urban approach, a methodology seemingly inspired by Italian Postmodernism, as seen in the work of Aldo Rossi, Vittorio Gregotti et al. There is a hint of the heavy, rationalist, super-urban construction of Gregotti's Stadio Luigi Ferraris in Genoa (1987–89), although there is little of his solidity in Taveira's oeuvre. Taveira's structures are composed of a series

of smaller volumes expressed individually within the overall plan and layout. It is an approach that was also picked up by the followers of the Germanic tradition of alternative, organic Modernism, from Hans Scharoun through to Günter Behnisch and Co-op Himmelb(l)au. But with Taveira's architecture there is none of the restraint or the sparse architectonic vocabulary of steel and glass that defines the German and Austrian traditions. Taveira uses colour, texture and surface to differentiate the elements, to create an internal aesthetic landscape. The design scheme for the Albufeira Marina Nautical Club, currently under construction, is intended to provide both outlook and urban presence, as a landmark defining the periphery of the marina. A series of sculptural, variegated, picturesque and often quite humorous forms constitutes the housing (with a vaguely Miami feel to it) while the apex of the scheme is a dramatic and crystalline seafood restaurant. The buildings take some influence from Gehry, but their architectonic vocabulary derives from the boats that will surround them in the marina development, their features referring to prows, sterns, bridges, masts and decks with railings appearing as balconies. From the rendering they are reminiscent of a collection of little vessels bumping and nudging each other with the gentle swell of the sea.

Aveiro Municipal Stadium

This extensive urban scheme is redeveloping a whole quarter, centred on the idea of sailing as a focus for the new community. The design drawings and studies reveal the design method, using computers to effectively sketch designs as models, creating complex 3D forms which interlock and create undulating, changeful townscapes.

Designs for the João Lagos Sports Complex show similar characteristics. Intended for Oeiras on the periphery of Lisbon, this brand new tennis centre incorporates a blend of the deconstructed, crystalline structures (a reminder of the German School) and the more familiar, highly coloured, toy-like elements. In Leões the sports complex is simpler and more coherent, the single volume of the arena expressed as a clear volume. This site is close to that intended for the João Lagos scheme, in Porto Salvo, Oeiras. The oval drum of the arena anchors the building to its site, visible from all angles. Its dark cladding differentiates it from the ancillary structures which are clad in variegated and brilliantly coloured tiles.

This use of coloured ceramic tiles, that is so clearly seen at the Barrô Social and Cultural Centre and the José Alvalade Stadium, is a revival of a Portuguese building tradition. The use of external tiles during the country's classical architectural period (from the sixteenth to the nineteenth centuries) is unusual and absolutely characteristic, a blend of influences drawn from Moorish, Ottoman, Spanish and Flemish traditions which spread through trade and expansion. In the twentieth century it was abandoned in favour of an International Style that eschewed surface decoration and colour. Tiling did, however, survive in the vernacular and the everyday as a short visit to the streets, bars and cafés of any of Portugal's cities or provincial towns will verify. People have customised their often bland and impersonal structures with brightly coloured, often geometrically patterned tiles. Portuguese quarters and Portuguese-influenced townscapes throughout the world from Rio de Janeiro to Toronto display this architectural customis-ation, the tiled vernacular. The current crop of Portuguese Modernists, Siza and those influenced by him, have adopted tiles in their architecture but have tended towards white or grey ceramics, working within the colour system of the International Style. Taveira, however, has resurrected the tradi-tion, but in a far from black and white version – in a populist patchwork of colour and culture. In the facades of Leões there is something of the way Gehry used the reflective titanium cladding at the Bilbao Guggenheim. Where the Californian used sheet metal as a reference to an industrial tradition, to shipbuilding and to the glimmering surface of the water,

Aveiro Municipal Stadium

TAVEIRA
SPORTS
ARCHITECTURE

Taveira prefers to use ceramic tiles to evoke a popular tradition that creates both adornment and signature.

The Barrô complex in northern Portugal was sponsored by Adolfo Roque, Portugal's largest ceramics manufacturer, who was born and brought up in Barrô. The centre's garish tiled facades, a riot of colour and collapsing, crumpling forms, help anchor it into the community.

In the case of the impressive Leiria stadium, the undulating roof seems to echo the hills that form a backdrop to the building, while the exquisite lightness of the structure contrasts with the solidity of a castle that nestles on a hilltop in the distance. A gap created between the roof and the back of the stadium allows light in from the rear (as well as that coming from above through the clear roof) while the roof itself appears to be floating above the seating. The smoothness of the scheme is enhanced by incorporating the lighting into the front edge of the roof, making it a multifunctional structure. Pylons supporting the roof are barely visible from within so that the effect of a snaking, continuous, self-supporting canopy is enhanced. Here, as at the José Alvalade and Aveiro Municipal stadia, the seating is coloured to simulate a fuller stadium in the absence of big crowds, an anti-climax which seems inevitable after the Euro 2004 tournament.

Aveiro's Municipal Stadium sports a similarly slick roof. Here its elevation above the solidity of the stands is even more pronounced. The facilities are assembled in a series of individual blocks set deliberately outside the curtilage defined by the roof. They are reminiscent of the micro-cities envisaged by Aldo Rossi and his Italian contemporaries with their obsession with the memory of urban archetypes. Unusually for the genre, Taveira's stadia all refer to the urban condition, even when sited at desolate or suburban locations. There is a consistency in his designs – to maintain the stadium as an urban fragment, as the successor to the Colosseum and the Roman arena, while never losing sight of the populism and quirky, decorative approach that have become his trademark. His buildings become those dreamt of city archetypes, despite their often provincial, often distinctly unpromising locations.

Aldo Rossi, in his essay 'Architettura e citta: passato e presente' (1972), wrote:
'As an architect I have never had a clearer understanding of Roman architecture than when I saw the Roman theatre and aqueduct in Budapest [Aquincum]; where these ancient elements are set deep in a busy industrial zone, where the Roman theatre is a football field for local boys and where a crowded tramway crosses the remains of the aqueduct.

Aveiro Municipal Stadium

Obviously these images, this use of the monument, is not generally to be advised; but it invites a compositional vision of the ancient elements within the city which is certainly not that of the city as museum.'

As it happens, Rossi is mistaken about the theatre. The structure he refers to at Aquincum is a Roman stadium. The boys playing football are, in reality, fulfilling its destiny, although they are probably not aware of how appropriate their game is. The football stadium and the Roman arena are different manifestations of the same thing; the container for the passion, elation, disappointment and collective release that make sports architecture an indispensable element in the architecture of cities, both in the past and now.

Architecture and Sport

In an age where communities are becoming fragmented, where personal contact is rarer and public space is slowly becoming less public and less centripetal, the stadium is becoming an increasingly pivotal public arena, an outlet for mass emotion. Television and the electronic media are alienating and isolating individuals. Sport's role in bringing people together is now seen as a vital constituent of contemporary culture. An audience in a theatre affects the atmosphere and the perception of drama or music. In sport, and in football in particular, the crowd is an essential part of the spectacle and an indispensable element in the ritual. 'Home advantage' is down to the huge boost of the friendly crowd but it is also, in part, dependent on the architecture, the crowd's container. The paradox with football is that even the very finest stadium is not the ideal vehicle for watching the game.

Rein Jansma, founding partner with Moshe Zwarts of Zwarts and Jansma Architecten who designed the Feyenoord stadium (Van den Broek Bakema) and the New Spartan and Galganwaard stadia, has said:
'The challenge is, that when all's said and done, a football stadium is a completely useless building because you're much better off watching football on television. It's a building dedicated to the emotion of "being there". An incredible amount of money is reserved for a stadium that is only used once a week for a couple of hours maximum. It's a marvellous challenge to design a building for this phenomenon. On top of this more and more functions have been clustered in the stadium in recent years and this makes the building more complex. People have come to understand that it's actually rather a shame to go to the stadium only to leave it again after the match.'

Aveiro Municipal Stadium

Zwarts and Jansma's recent designs for Utrecht's Stadion Galganwaard, a coherent and elegant proposal to update the original structure which dates from the late 1970s, have been presaged in many key features by the architecture of Tomás Taveira. The masts or structural pylons, the individually expressed yet contiguous roofs and also the integration of urban architecture (including a pair of office blocks built at the corners with views on to the pitch) into the stadium are design devices used by Taveira at Benfica, Leiria and Faro.

Bob Lang, associate director of Ove Arup, the internationally renowned engineers of the Hong Kong stadium, Lord's mound stand in London and the Ellis Park stadium in Johannesburg among others, has said:
'In Classical architecture terms – the form and function argument – stadia are hugely functional places. There are strict rules of safety and organisation and out of that rigour a certain number of design options evolve.'

It is the functional aspects of stadium design that intrigue Taveira. 'What influenced me,' he says, 'were the types of comfort and facilities you need to encourage you out of your home together with your beautiful wife and your beautiful children. To get you out without you having to suffer from the cold and discomfort, that there are restaurants and places to eat and drink. In a way it should be comparable to a theatre where you need to be able to see the smallest details of the complexions of the actors. Only in the stadium you need to be so close to the game that you are almost able to smell the sweat on the skin of the players. Comfort is the most important thing; the flow of information to the audience, the convenience of transportation to the site and the security inside and out.'

Designed by Rob Schuurman and Sjoerd Soeters in 1993, undoubtedly the apex of luxury for the masses is the Amsterdam ArenA, a multi-purpose structure accommodating sports and events with varying levels of service and comfort. Use of a curious, eclectic blend of Postmodernism and straightforward structural Rationalism leads to architecture which would look at home in the semi-industrial docks of Amsterdam or Rotterdam. 'The ArenA,' says Taveira, 'is an important influence. It is a highly comfortable, highly

Aveiro Municipal Stadium

enjoyable stadium, full of restaurants and excellent facilities and more like a family entertainment centre. You could stay there, and want to stay there, all day.' Schuurman and Soeters' building is bold in its use of colour. This, too, is an idea they have in common with Taveira.

Taveira is well known for his love of colour and extravagant use of brilliant ceramics. At the José Alvalade Stadium he employs his characteristic explosion of colour on the seats, creating a variegated background which mirrors the brilliant colours of the facades. 'These buildings have been conceived for the Euro 2004 football tournament. When it is over they will stand more than half-empty again. At a big match at Sporting Lisbon we may get attendances of 20,000. The smaller teams are often lucky to get crowds of 1,000. The colours help to inhabit them.'

'Even those stadia which exist as beautiful objects,' Taveira continues, 'can be a bit dull. I'm totally against the pure white of Rationalism. I need buildings to be clad in happiness!'

What Taveira has achieved is all the more remarkable considering the restrictive budgets to which he has been working, budgets which are dwarfed by the familiar big international stadia of recent years from the Olympic venues to the Stade de France. 'I was always very constrained by cost,' Taveira explains. 'Our budgets were poor, our materials were poor. Every bit of money was under scrutiny, sometimes, of course, we have to be constrained and under scrutiny. But I'm happy with the results we achieved under those conditions.'

All successful sports structures depend entirely on their ability to become containers of atmosphere. A plethora of functional and environmental requirements are needed to meet contemporary expectations and regulations. These can be calculated by computers; they are the result of tables, and engineers' mathematics and programmes. What cannot be calculated in advance is that magic spark, the atmosphere, that unreliable chimera which depends on another unpredictable factor: the crowd. The Euro 2004 football tournament will soon testify to the success of Taveira's stadia; it is the crowds, a rich mix of locals and tourists, who will decide their fate.

Architecture Interpreting Sport

During the last fifty years popular sports such as football, tennis and athletics have witnessed huge growth in sports-related industries. In the 1950s professional teams held matches in privately owned stadia or arenas where team managers and owners preferred not to become involved with the public. This often led to a shortfall in funding with little chance to provide better equipment or training facilities. Teams who turned to their local council for help were often disappointed by the lack of interest, and some chose to re-locate to another region or state where they could find the backing they required. When corporations were approached for sponsorship the world of sport took a huge leap forward. Corporations quickly realised the potential of marketing their products to capacity crowds, added to which the increase in televised events meant potential audiences of millions.

Sport has now become a global industry; the final decades of the last millennium furthered international expansion and sports club systems around the world leading to an internationalisation of sport business activities. The knock-on effect of all this is that players have become significantly more competitive in their efforts to qualify against the best in the world. This in turn has made players, teams and their managers into celebrities both at home and abroad. The venue that hosts a sporting event is now expected be of an equal calibre; it must add to the thrill of the physical action, becoming a theatre for the audience.

Many larger grounds acknowledge this simply in their names, Stadium of Light, Theatre of Dreams and so on. Satellite links around the world are able to bring the Olympics, the World Cup and Wimbledon into our homes. Getting a live audience into the stadia and arenas has required these buildings to change, to become more ambitious in their scale and the level of comfort and entertainment they can offer. In some cases there is a demand for other activities within the building to keep all members of the family amused during the course of a game.

Often facilities such as exhibition halls or conference rooms have been incorporated as flexible usage helps to

Maggie Toy

keep the structure economically viable. Stadia and sports halls are now seen as excellent spaces to host large convivial functions for corporations or private individuals. As a consequence, architects have had to step up their product and design facilities that outclass the competitors. Innovations have included entire football pitches that slide underneath the auditorium, vast folding roofs and telescopic stands able to increase or decrease the amount of seating. It is no longer just the sport itself that is expected to demonstrate the staging of world-class skills, it is also the venue.

Cities from every part of the planet vie with one another to host world championships. Once chosen, there follows a long programme of construction and regeneration to provide stadia that will be considered exemplary by the rest of the world. Major international sports occasions can command the building of several sporting arenas for just a single event.

In the north of England, Manchester hosted the 2002 Commonwealth Games. The regeneration programme left the city with an impressive new ground for local football teams,

the completion of an entirely new transport system, and improved shopping facilities, concert halls and museums. This architectural facelift brought benefits not only to the sporting community but to the city as a whole, by generating new jobs and encouraging tourism.

The chance of improving whole economies acts like a magnet to potential hosts – staging is expensive but the financial and social rewards to be gained are compelling. Football/soccer is another example of this phenomenon. The 2002 World Cup in Japan demonstrated to all stadia designers just what could be achieved. These stadia masterpieces were works of art, not only for football but for their continuous use and contribution to the cities.

The Euro 2004 tournament to be held in Portugal will be following suit. Portugal will use ten stadia at a total cost for building and regeneration work in excess of £300 million. It is expected, however, that Portugal will generate a similar amount from hosting the event. In addition to direct financial benefits there will be indirect profit. Such an important event

Dr. Magalhães Pessoa
Municipal Stadium, Leiria

is viewed around the world, bringing additional kudos, and advantageously highlighting Portugal's potential.

Possibly the most vital aspect to be considered during such a building programme is the ongoing use of the stadia after the event. Flexible, adaptable, environmentally friendly designs are the way forward and therefore more attention is being given to these structures so that they benefit all the community. All three stadia designed by Tomás Taveira – Aveiro Municipal Stadium, Dr. Magalhães Pessoa Municipal Stadium in Lieria and the José Alvalade Stadium in Lisbon – will earn their keep as home grounds after UEFA have left.

The Portuguese stadia are something to be proud of. Football Federation chief and organising-committee chairman Gilberto Madail expounds: 'There were doubts expressed about whether we could do what we promised to do and, painfully, a lot of those doubts came from within Portugal.' Madail goes on, 'What we've done is show that a small country is capable of achieving something spectacular.' A combination of Portuguese talent and internationally renowned

architects designed the impressive stadia for their locations.

Taveira's contribution to architecture in Portugal started in 1967, and since then he has consistently contributed to the architectural landscape of his homeland. His extensive experience covers large apartment blocks, social housing, banks, shopping centres, schools and urban-planning schemes, so it has been a natural progression for him to work on stadia and sports-related buildings.

A free-style architect, he works like an artist – he is receptive to styles of architecture from around the world which he then reinterprets through his own work. Very aware of the progress being made by architects on the international stage, he talks freely of the work of Greg Lynn, Reiser & Umemoto and FOA. Taveira's roots are with James Stirling, Michael Graves and the Smithsons. There is a clear empathy with the work of Frank Gehry and it is not difficult to draw similarities in his massing of finished physical forms. Both he and Gehry are connected by their belief in imagination and the rejection of prejudice. He believes that Gehry's forms are essentially

Aveiro Municipal Stadium

Baroque in origin, and that this is an aesthetic perfectly adapted to current architecture. Taveira admires flexibility of mind, a mind open to investigation and adventure, and his architecture certainly demonstrates what he admires!

According to Taveira, architecture is an art using the techniques of construction. He firmly believes that while the engineer has a key role to play in the creation of architecture, the architects themselves should have a thorough understanding of how the structure will work. Architects should not merely draw a concept, but work with the engineer to understand how to make it a reality. 'The architect has to be very conscious of how the structures work and how they may behave, in order for the connection between the two types of professionals to be advantageous,' says Taveira.

The stadia featured in this book demonstrate how this working relationship has been used to full effect. The very nature of the buildings sets intricate engineering challenges which have been met by this two-way understanding of the working process that Taveira advocates.

In conclusion, the aspect of Taveira's work that sets him apart from other architects on the world stage is his dramatic and unashamed use of bold, bright colours to enhance the physical volumes. He loves colour and wants to share this love with the people for whom he is designing.

Historically, architecture in the Mediterranean, from ancient Greece and Rome to North Africa, was richly coloured. Taveira's use of colour, locally made ceramic tiles and glass in a sea of minimalist architecture shaded in monotones, is a creative revival of traditional materials and decoration now strikingly used to embellish very contemporary forms. His sports facilities make outstanding landmarks, eye-catching in their mantel of bright colours and textures, and exhilarating in their clever use of volumes and gravity-defying roofs.

He never forgets that his architecture is for the people; it has to perform for all their senses. Taveira has said that he wants the new club in Albufeira Marina to be 'welcoming' in its appearance, and it is this feeling of welcome and excitement that is the hallmark of all his buildings.

José Alvalade Stadium, Lisbon

The José Alvalade Stadium was intended to be unique among current Portuguese stadia. This competition design for the Euro 2004 football tournament was a compromise between football and its requirements, on a site that would also include a 4-storey sports centre (with a gymnasium and a 25-metre swimming pool), health club – possibly the largest in Portugal – a family entertainment centre, restaurants, cinemas, bowling, shops, a sports museum, the Portugal Sporting Club megastore and a head office.

The site covers 52,317 square metres and is approximately 10 kilometres north of the heart of Lisbon, in a housing area known as Alvalade. There are good communication links with existing roads and an underground system. The stadium's 7 storeys, some of which are underground, seat a capacity audience of 50,000 including seats and facilities exclusively for the disabled. Extensive subterranean parking (approximately 3,630 spaces) lies beneath the pitch. In the event of an emergency, there are tunnels from this subterranean area below floor -3, which lead directly to the exits.

Two towers house elevators and stairways for VIPs, the press and media. The shape of the roof, supported only by 4 masts, is a direct derivation of the stadium volumetric, giving a wave effect. Precast concrete panels have been used for the facades and these are covered with ceramic tiles depicting the emblem for the Portugal Sporting Club: a green and yellow background surmounted by a lion.

Inside, coloured tiles help to identify facilities – for example, bars and toilets. The stadium is designed to be as colourful as possible both inside and out, including the myriad-coloured seating, giving the appearance that the stadium is always crowded. The country's good climate ensures natural light in abundance, but when artificial lighting is necessary care has been taken to prevent glare affecting players, spectators and photographic equipment.

The stadium caters magnificently for the public, allowing a visit to the stadium to become a day out. There are 3 restaurants, and VIP boxes have their own catering services. In the adjacent buildings are 43 bars, and a shopping mall with cinemas and 32 shops.

José Alvalade Stadium, Lisbon

Initial roof scheme

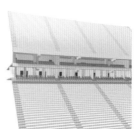

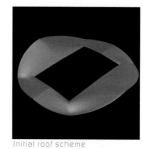

Initial roof scheme

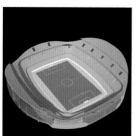

Initial scheme showing four
rings of stands

Second floor plan

Study of floodlighting

Study of the skyboxes

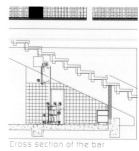

Cross section of the bar

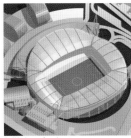

Initial roof scheme

Study of floodlighting

Initial roof scheme

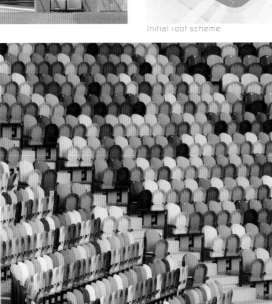

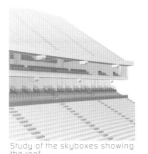

Study of the skyboxes showing the roof

Study of the skyboxes from the stands

Study of the skyboxes

José Alvalade Stadium, Lisbon

José Alvalade Stadium, Lisbon

José Alvalade Stadium, Lisbon

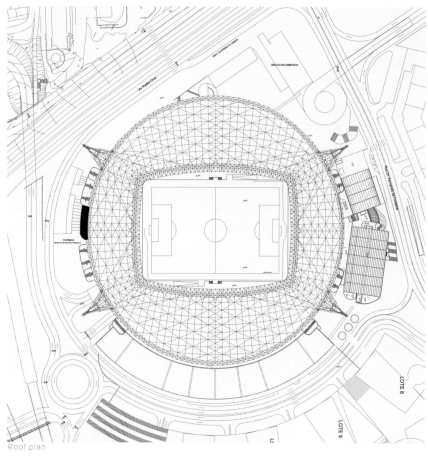

Roof plan

Initial roof scheme

Detail of the multi-sports building

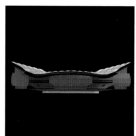

Initial roof scheme

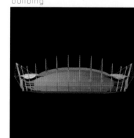

Initial roof scheme

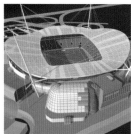

Initial roof scheme, also health club and multi-sports buildings

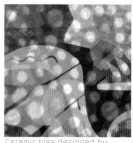

Ceramic tiles designed by Ricardo Taveira

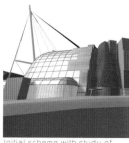

Initial scheme with study of multi-sports building

Initial scheme with volumetric study of the health club, multi-sports and headquarters buildings

The multi-sports building

Initial roof scheme, also health club and multi-sports buildings

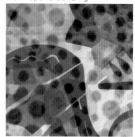

Ceramic tiles designed by Ricardo Taveira

Initial scheme with study of the health club

South-east view

Initial scheme with volumetric study of the health club and multi-sports buildings

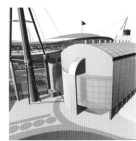

The multi-sports building

The multi-sports building

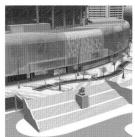

Shopping centre entrance

South-east view

VIP access tower

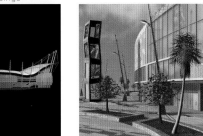

Initial roof scheme

The shopping centre

Initial roof scheme and volumetric study

Tile scheme for the toilets

Detail of the mast

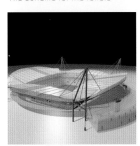

Initial roof scheme and volumetric study

José Alvalade Stadium, Lisbon

Initial scheme for the south elevation

Initial scheme for the west elevation

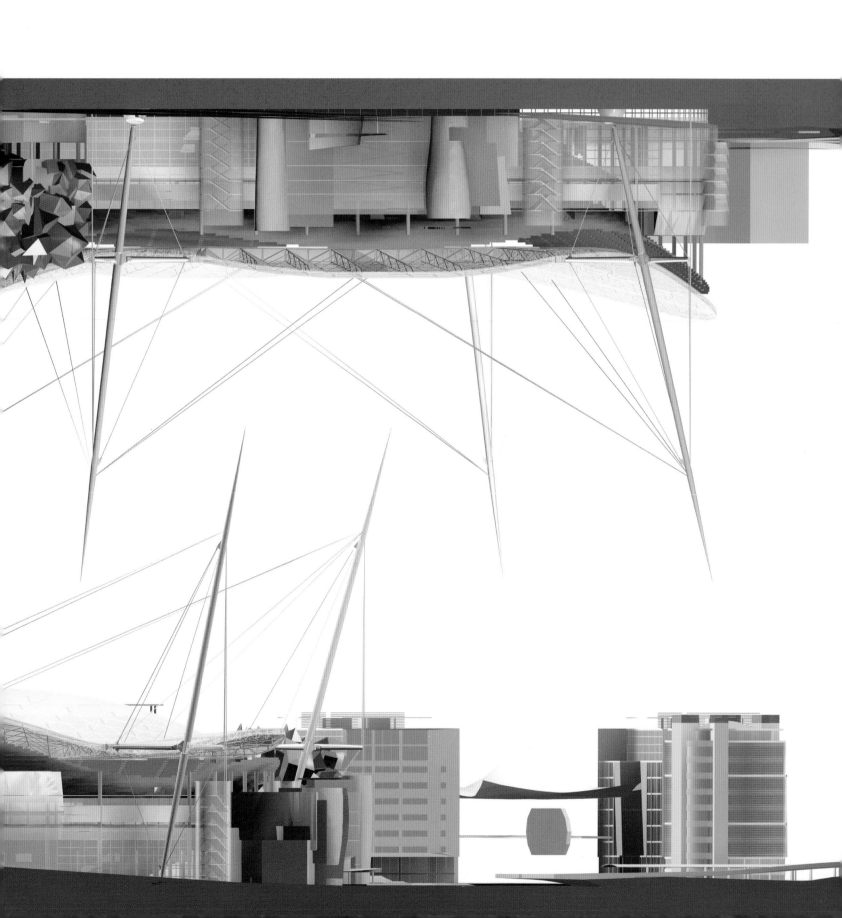

Initial scheme

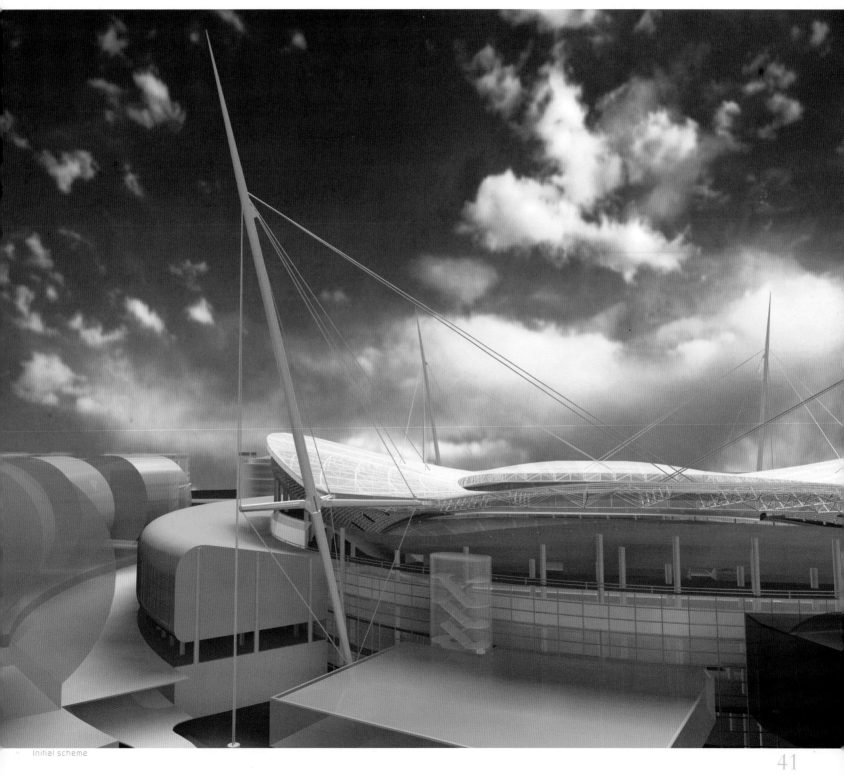

Initial scheme

José Alvalade Stadium, Lisbon

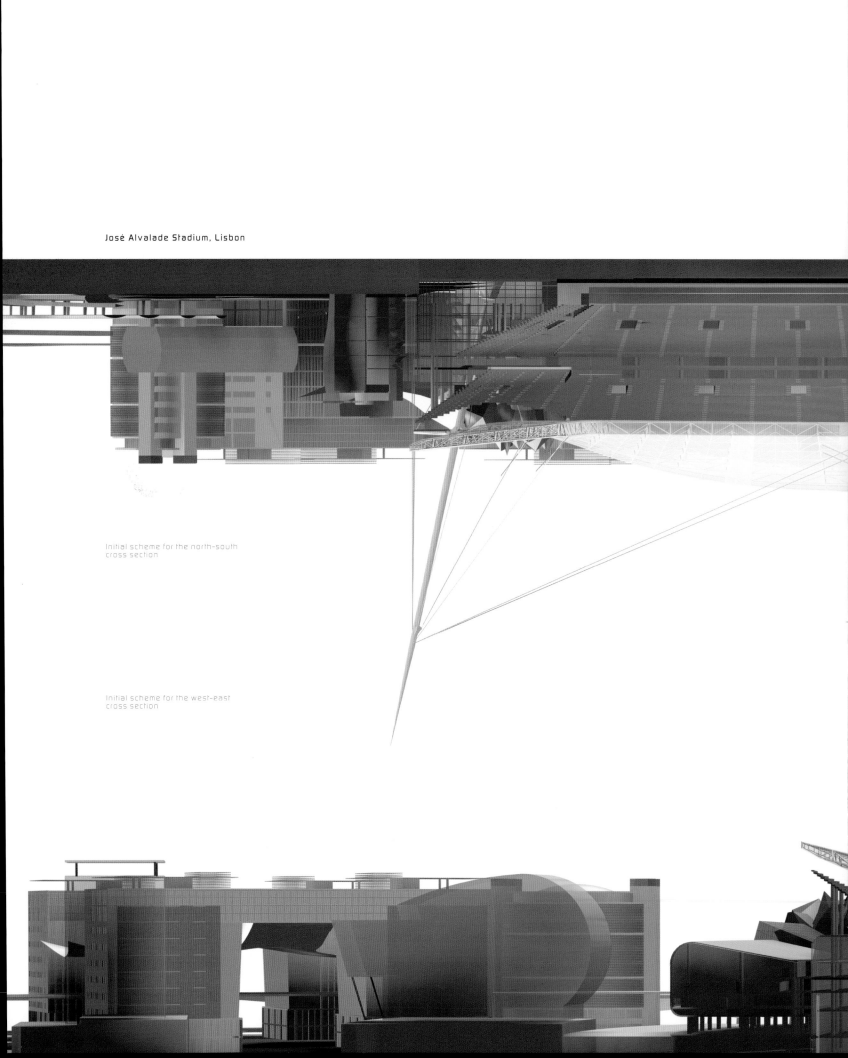

Initial scheme for the north-south
cross section

Initial scheme for the west-east
cross section

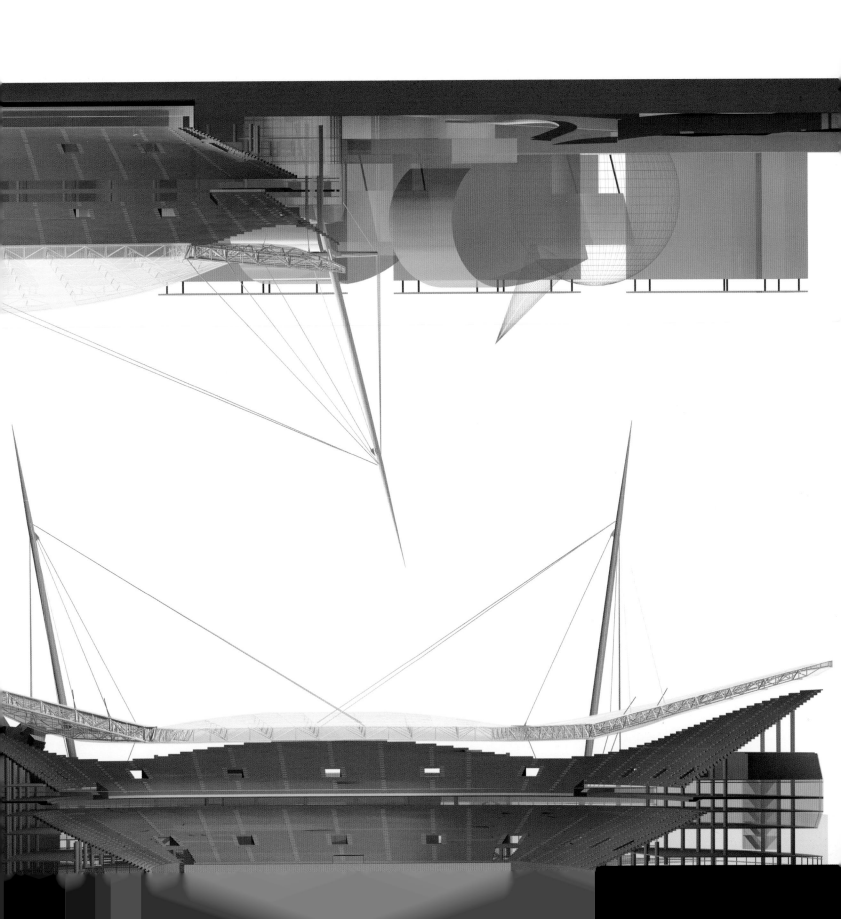

José Alvalade Stadium, Lisbon

Alvalade XXI
ESTÁDIO JOSÉ ALVALADE

VIP access tower

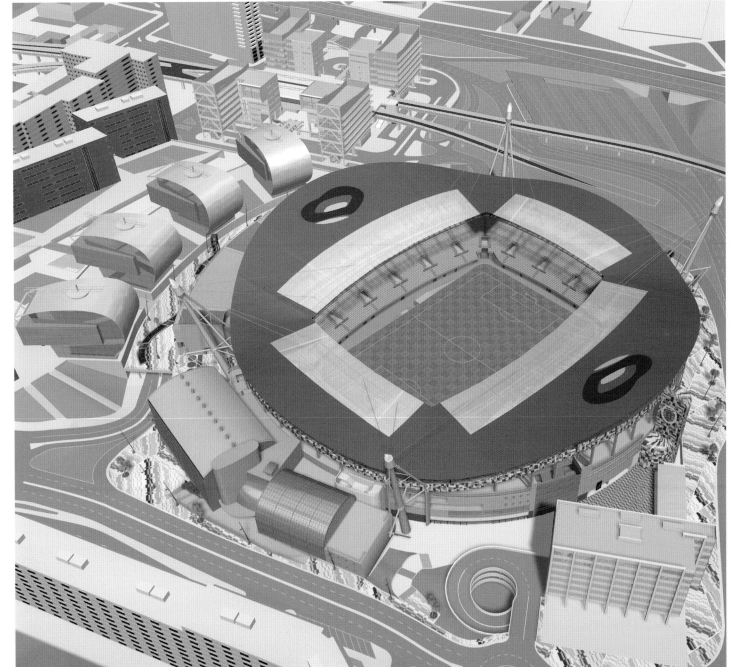

Aerial view

José Alvalade Stadium, Lisbon

South elevation

East elevation

West elevation

José Alvalade Stadium, Lisbon

Health club reception area

Press conference room

Public access and control

Access to stands

Health club access area

Health club reception area

Initial scheme for VIP shopping area

Press conference room

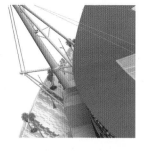
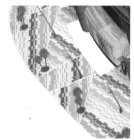

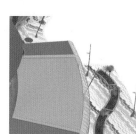

Changing rooms access area

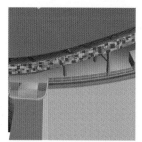

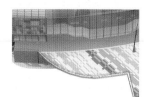
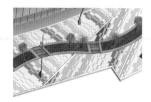

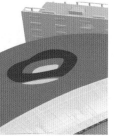

Aveiro Multi-Sports Centre

Nestled on the southern shore of a marshy lagoon Aveiro, some 250 kilometres north of Lisbon, is also known as 'little Venice' because of the many canals that go through this seaside city. The competiton programme for a site of 52,733 square metres requested a sports venue which complied with Portuguese professional sports regulations, able to host indoor sports including basketball, volleyball, tennis, boxing and athletics with a minimum seating capacity of 4,000 spectators. At the same time it should easily convert into a much-needed congress hall where cultural events, exhibitions, theatre productions or even large dances could be held.

The completed centre has 4 storeys and is capable of seating 7,465 spectators (including the disabled). There are telescopic stands and 11 skyboxes. The refreshment facilities located at levels 1 and 3 include 2 restaurants and 9 bars. Shops can be found in the VIP entrance area. Space designated for the media is large enough to accommodate a minimum of 40 journalists, and includes a comfortable meeting room and a further interview room for radio or television presenters.

In an attempt to add an element of excitement to the city the new building was designed to rupture the uniformity of existing architecture. Heavy precast concrete has been used for the structure to contrast with the stadium roof. Constructed from steel and polycarbonate sheets the roof has a lightweight quality, and rather resembles a long-playing record which has been slipped at an angle over the top of the building. This incline creates 2 stands of different heights in the interior space, the higher stand being reserved for the media, VIPs and presidential skyboxes. The exterior curve of the roof extends over the entrance to provide a canopy. Walls and roof are accentuated in bold colours giving further vibrancy to the design.

All sporting activities are accommodated on the pitch and athletics track. The telescopic stands and elevated stage make the space even more flexible than was originally required in the brief, allowing a wide variety of events to take place. The disabled and their companions have been designated the exclusive use of 226 seats and indoor parking spaces.

Roof

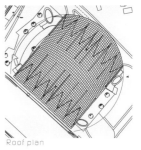
Roof plan

Level +3

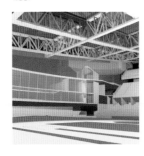

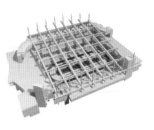
Roof system

Level +1

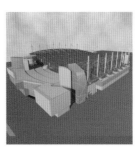
Level +4

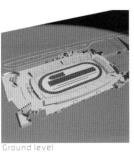
Ground level

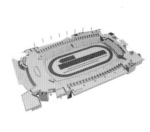

Level +2

Level -1

Faro/Loulé Intermunicipal Stadium

This was a competition entry for the Euro 2004 foot-ball tournament. The stadium had to fulfil all FIFA regulations and be able to seat 30,000 spectators. Also to be included were 500 VIP- and bus-parking spaces, a helicopter pad and large landscaped areas for the use of visitors, all on a site of 12 hectares.

Faro is on the coast of southern Portugal. The city is the administrative centre for the whole Algarve region and has a population of 60,000 clustered in the small pedestrian streets around the port and marina. A key issue for the site of the stadium in Faro was the direction of the sun and the integration of the stadium on the flattest part of the hilly site. It was decided that the best solution would be to distribute the stadium over 2 rings. The symmetrical stadium then had its seating prefabricated with a repetition of elements.

Similar in construction to the roof of the Aveiro and Sporting Club stadia, the metallic roof is a light structure covered with steel and polycarbonate sheets with lighting equipment placed at its inner edge. There are 7 storeys, including 2 basements. An adjoining building, off-limits to the general public, provides accommodation for players, referees, physicians and delegates as well as areas designated for VIP restaurants, bars and special skyboxes.

Concrete, polycarbonate and metal were employed in construction, while the facades of the stadium and the VIP building to the west of the site use prefabricated panels interspersed with elements of glass and metallic mesh. Everything has to be easily maintained and built to last. The pitch is protected by a moat, the dimensions of which allow greater intimacy between spectators and players. It also acts as a through route for the circulation of lorries when the stadium is used for live concerts or large events.

After the tournament seating can be reduced to 20,000–22,000 or less simply by dismantling either the north or south stands, or both. The roof can also be dismantled in a similar manner if so required.

Faro/Loulé Intermunicipal Stadium

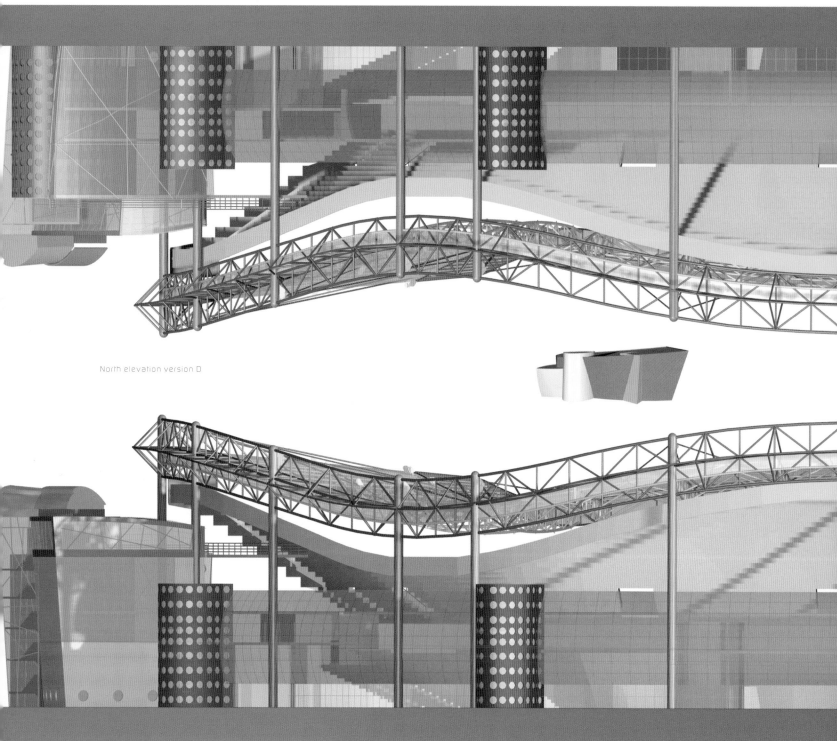

North elevation version D

South elevation version D

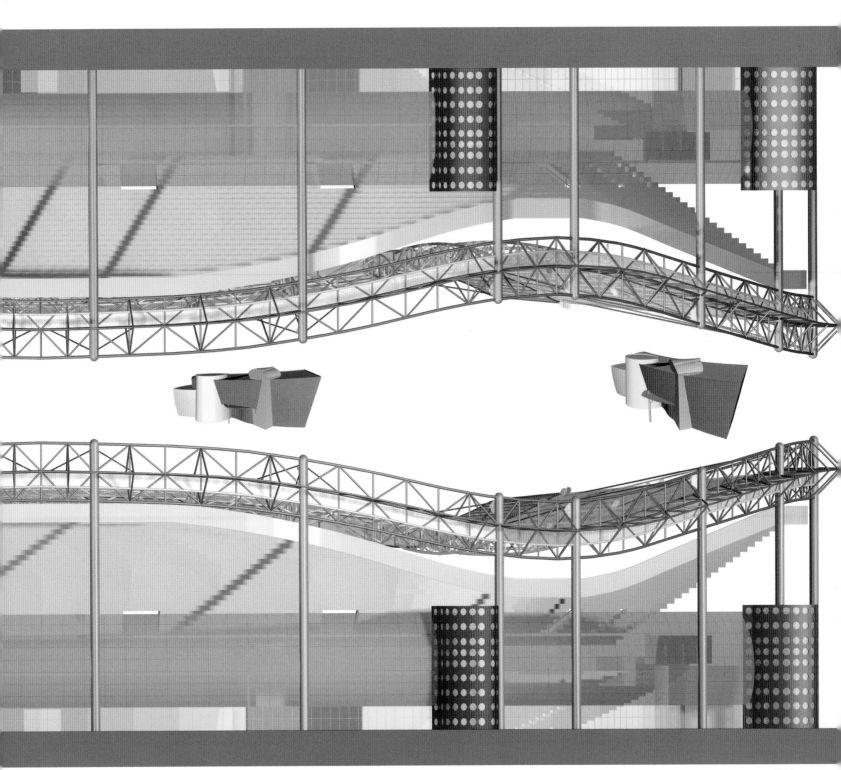

Faro/Loulé Intermunicipal Stadium

Four versions of the design scheme:

A With hotel on south area

B With hotel on south area covered by the stadium roof

C With hotel on south area without the north stands

D Without hotel and with all the stands

Hotel view

South-west view, version D

Preliminary study

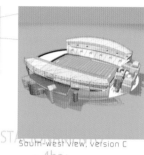

South-west view, version C

Hotel view from inside the stadium, version B

Hotel view

South-west view, version D

Preliminary study

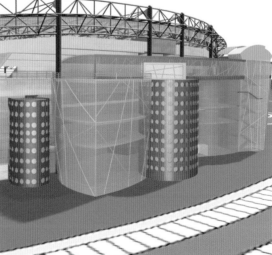

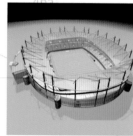

North-east view, version D

Main entrance

Hotel view

West-east cross section

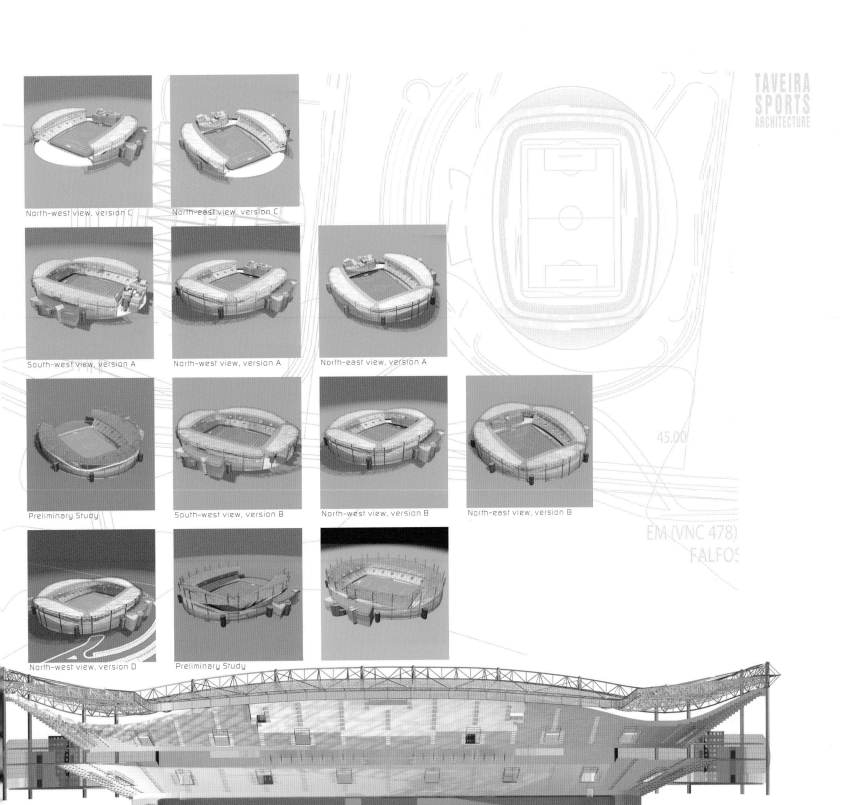

North-west view, version C

North-east view, version C

South-west view, version A

North-west view, version A

North-east view, version A

Preliminary Study

South-west view, version B

North-west view, version B

North-east view, version B

North-west view, version D

Preliminary Study

South-north cross section

TAVEIRA
SPORTS
ARCHITECTURE

45.00

EM (VNC 478)
FALFOS

59

Faro/Loulé Intermunicipal Stadium

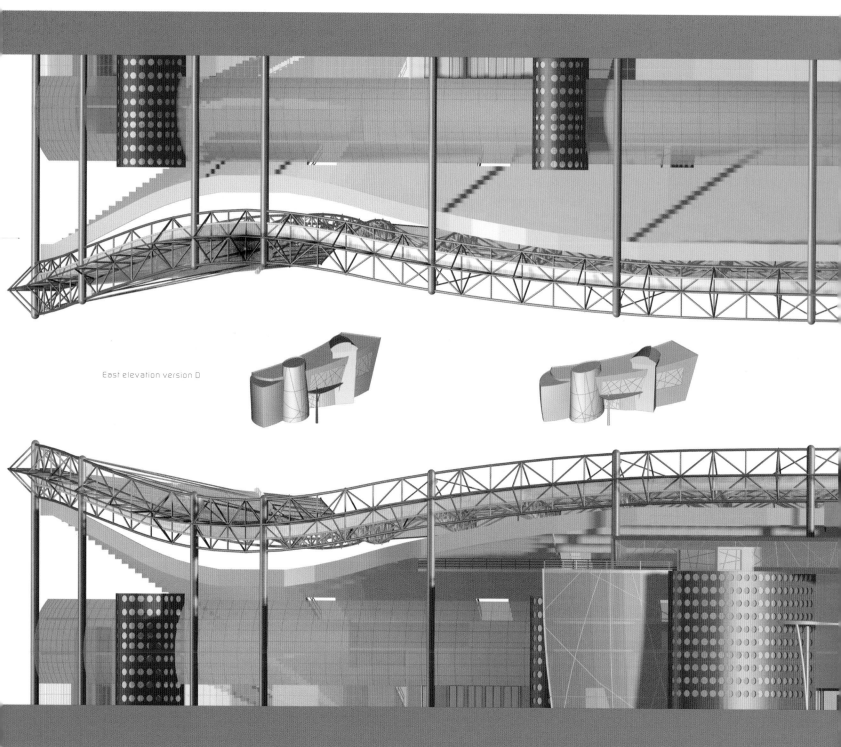

East elevation version D

West elevation version D

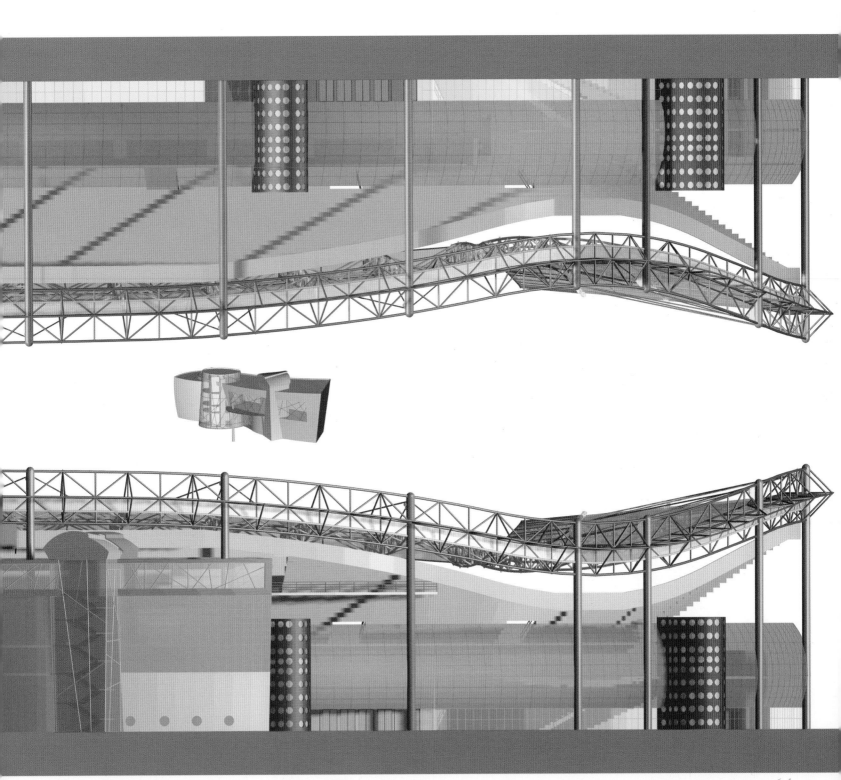

Sport Lisbon and Benfica Stadium (refurbishment)

Initially the request was for a refurbishment of the existing 77,000-seat home ground of Sport Lisbon and Benfica for the Euro 2004 football tournament. This meant a new roof for the stands, new dressing rooms for 4 teams and new commercial areas. Originally built in 1957, the stadium had been enlarged in 1978 and was still in relatively good condition so the predicted improvements seemed completely justifiable.

Today a football stadium is also a space for conviviality. The inclusion of 180 new skyboxes equipped with 2,000 business seats would help the stadium in its new role as a venue for corporate business functions by providing accommodation for VIP occasions.

The new facade on the existing stadium would be 'supported' by the existing concrete structure, with any existing brick walls being demolished and replaced by metallic grids and glass, giving a more 'high tech' look. A new roof would allow more natural light and ventilation into interior spaces. Constructed over the stands and supported by 13 masts, the roof would not touch the building at all. Tyrants coming from each mast and ending near the roof's inner limit would support it. Each mast would also be an access nucleus for 2 staircases and 2 elevators.

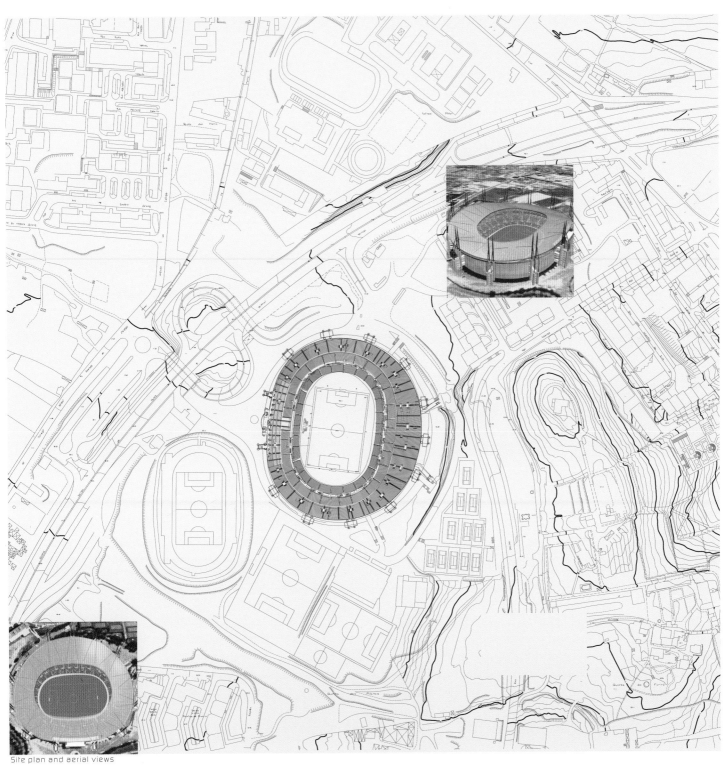

Site plan and aerial views

Sport Lisbon and Benfica Stadium (refurbishment)

North-west view

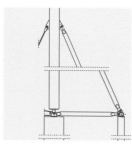

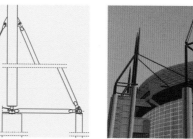

Skybox cross section

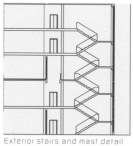

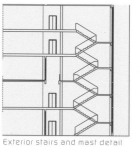

Exterior stairs and mast detail

Main entrance

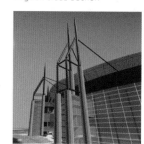

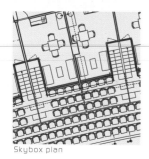

Skybox plan

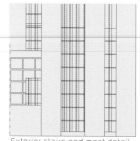

Exterior stairs and mast detail

North-east view

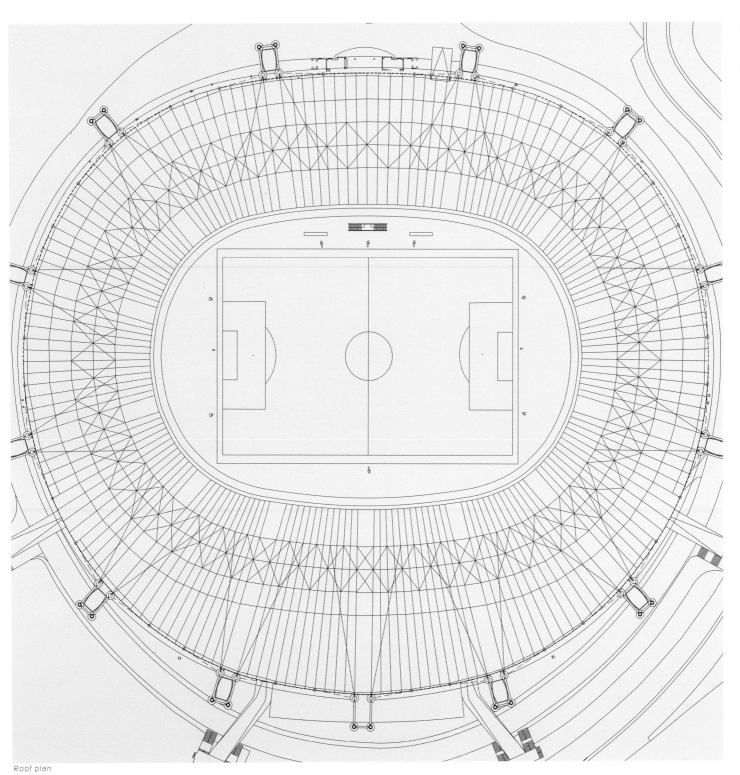

Roof plan

Sport Lisbon and Benfica Stadium (refurbishment)

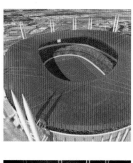

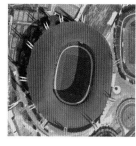

West entrance

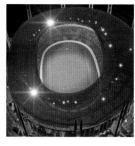

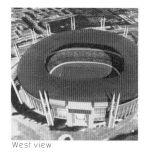

West view

North-west view

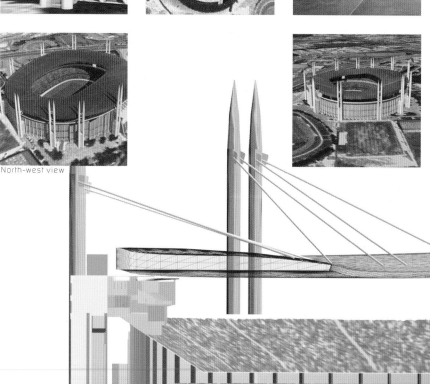

West-east cross section

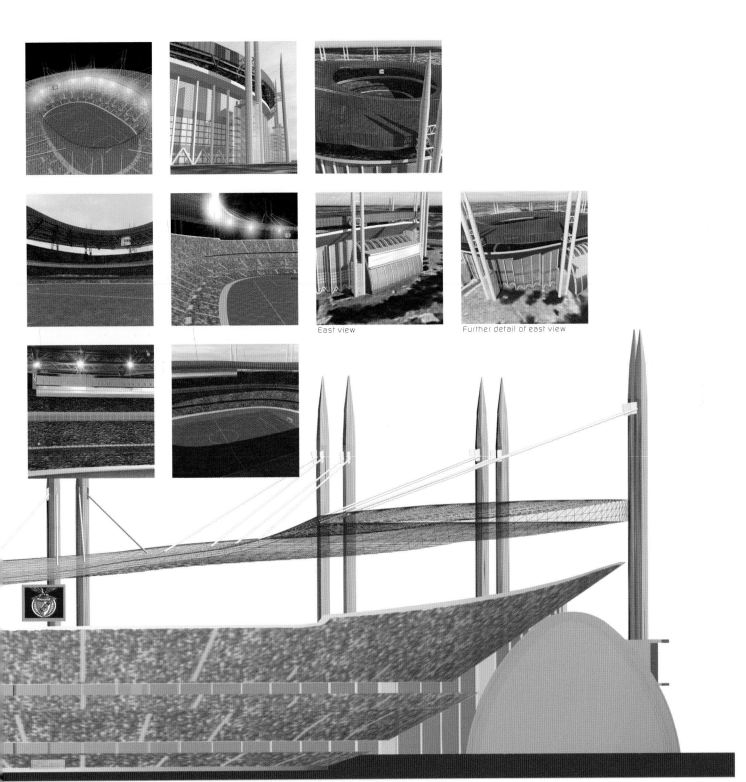

East view

Further detail of east view

Sport Lisbon and Benfica Stadium (refurbishment)

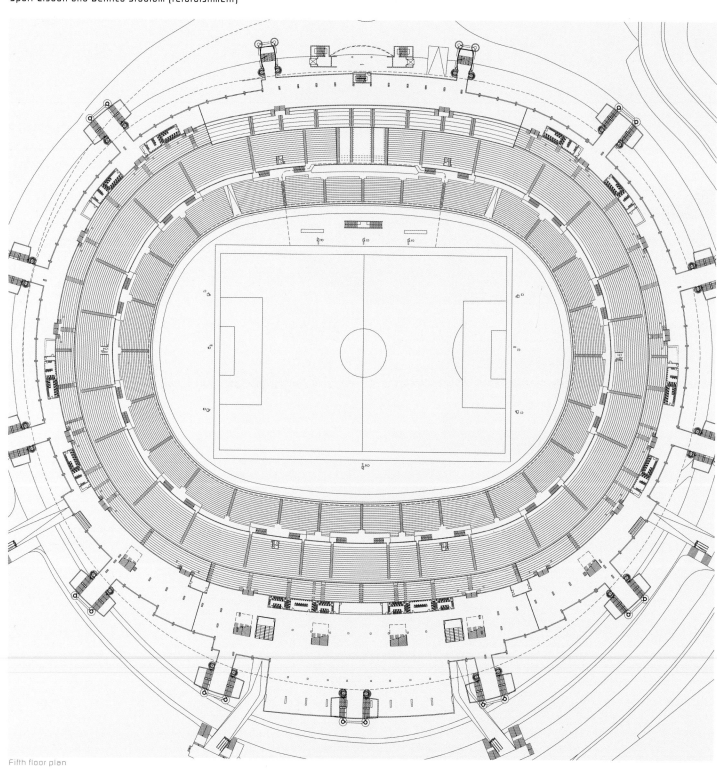

Fifth floor plan

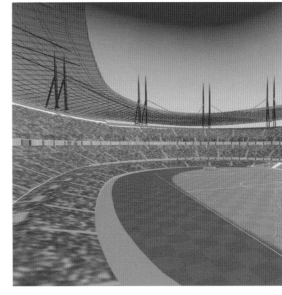

Interior views of skybox

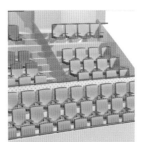

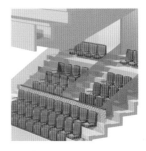

South-west view

Interior views of skybox

Sport Lisbon and Benfica Stadium (new)

Because other major clubs were building new stadia for the Euro 2004 tournament, Sport Lisbon and Benfica decided to rebuild their own stadium. Of all the stadia we have designed to this day, this is the only one with 4 rings. The first 2 rings are separated from the third and fourth by a line of skyboxes.

This stadium has a diameter of 180 metres, allowing spectators to sit closer to the matches which helps to create a very exciting atmosphere. The building has 8 storeys, including 2 basements, and seats 51,173 with a moat that can be used by transport bringing in heavy equipment, or 56,635 without the moat.

Building materials include precast concrete, glass, metallic structures and Teflon for the roof. Teflon is a translucent material that is both light and strong. The support structure for the roof is achieved with the help of pillars to which tyrants are attached. The form and lightness of the building are like that of a bird, specifically an eagle, which, by analogy, is the symbol of the club. Indoor car-parking space is provided for 458 vehicles; all other parking is outside. Other facilities include 22 bars, 2 restaurants and 2 shops.

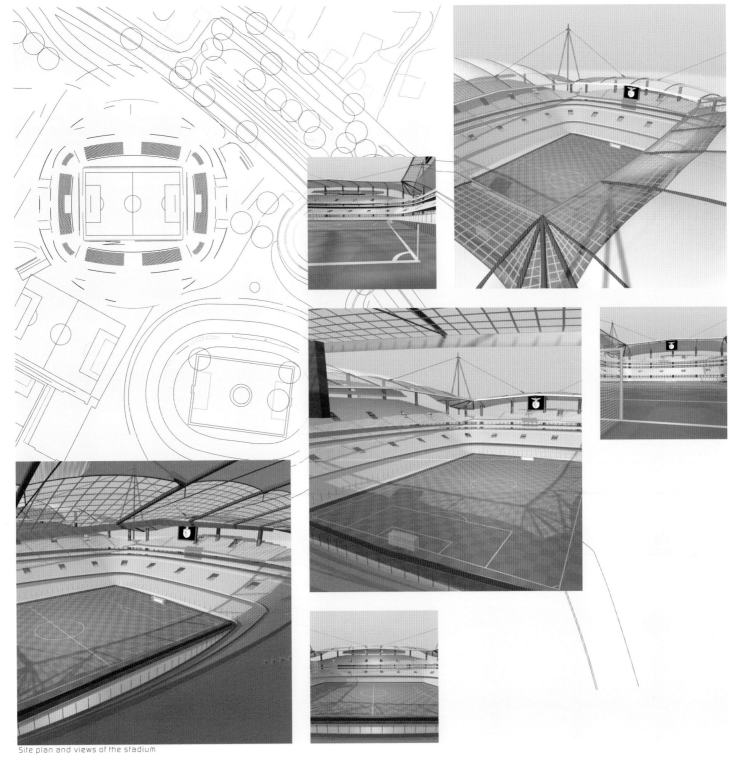

Site plan and views of the stadium

Sport Lisbon and Benfica Stadium (new)

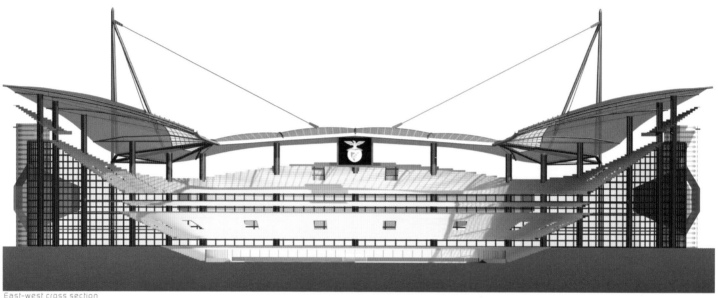

East-west cross section

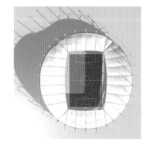
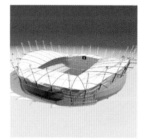
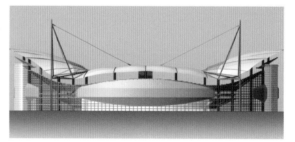
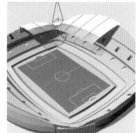

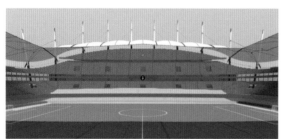
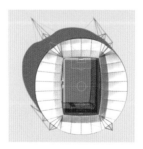
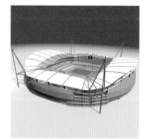

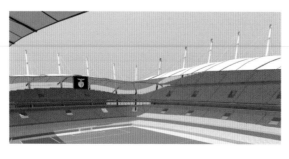
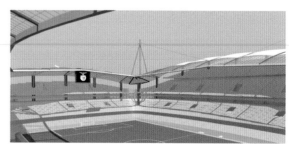

Views showing two versions of
the roof

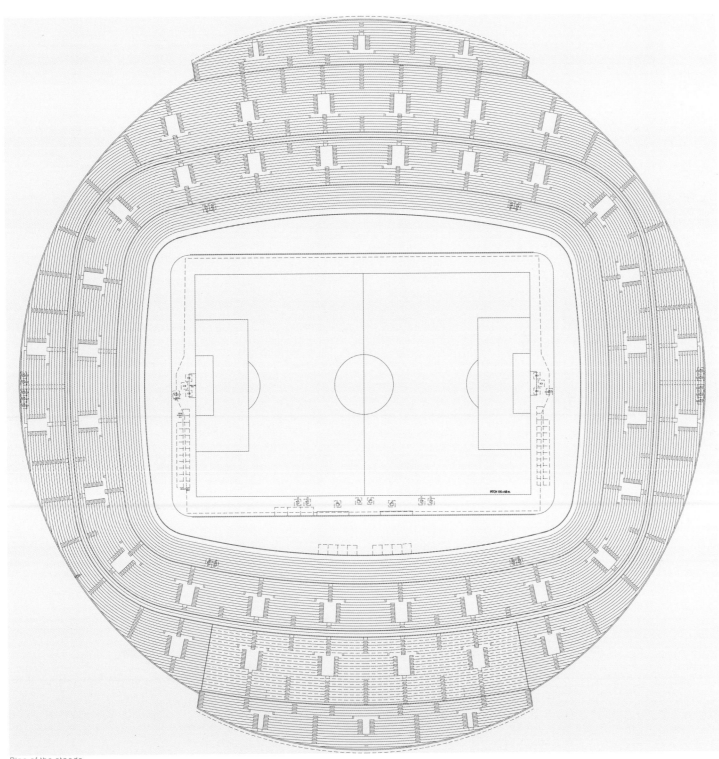

PITCH 105 x 68 m.

Plan of the stands

Sport Lisbon and Benfica Stadium (new)

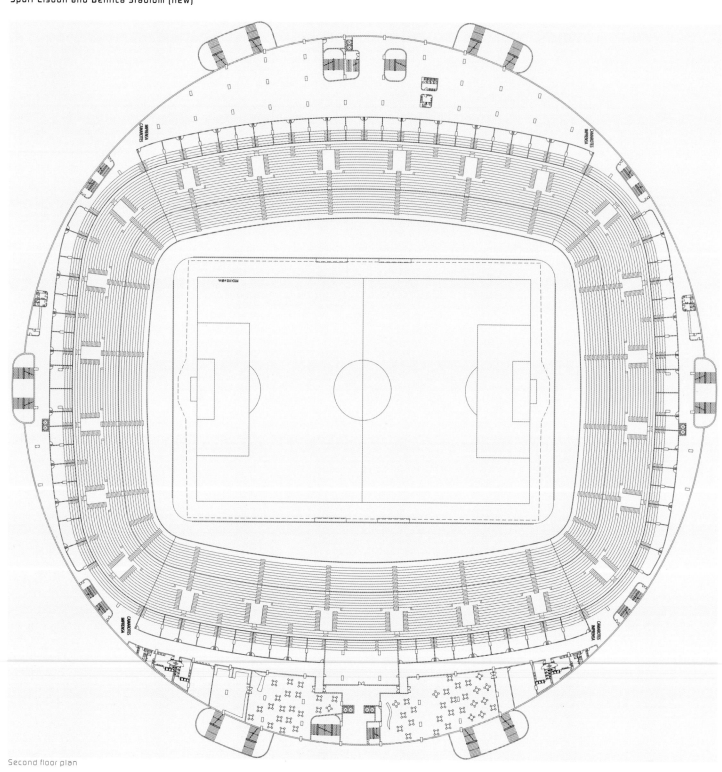

Second floor plan

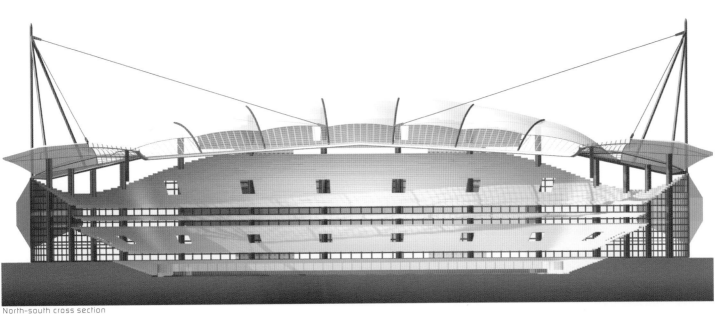

North-south cross section

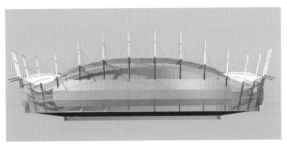
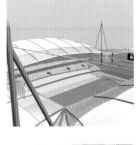

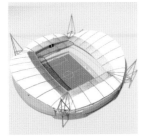
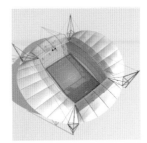
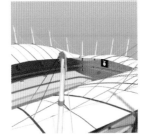
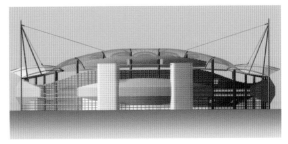

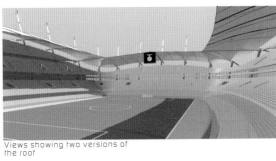
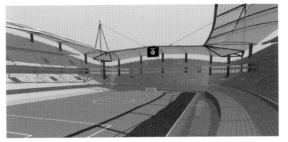
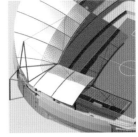

Views showing two versions of
the roof

Barrô Social and Cultural Centre

The idea for this centre derives from the energy and perseverance of Adolfo Roque, an architecture enthusiast. Roque was born in Barrô, a small community in Àgueda, northern Portugal. He is now an engineer and owner of the biggest ceramics enterprise in the country. He wanted to sponsor an architectural landmark in his home town that would completely disregard the prevailing rationalism in Portuguese architecture.

Located on an inclining street and surrounded by a few rural dwellings, the new centre has been laid out over 3 floors, forming a truncated pyramid with 'arms'. These 'arms' form 2 complementary zones: the first is dedicated to culture and includes a banqueting room and auditorium while the second houses a scouts headquarters, a coffee shop, a shop and the 'A Barca' head office.

The building becomes an outstanding feature anchored in its rural urban setting. There is a sense of deconstruction due to the inclination of the walls, but at the same time the entrance of light through skylights gives the feeling of a classical building. Finally, this curious free-style structure has been covered with a 'skin' of shiny ceramic tiles, composed into abstract geometric forms in different colours and dimensions by the architect Ricardo Taveira, giving a new twist to this traditional style of decoration.

Ceiling plan of ground floor

TAVEIRA
SPORTS
ARCHITECTURE

49.95

P5   P5

P5

I.S.F.
A=6.90m2

I.S.M.
A=6.90m2   P5

P4

P4

P4

Insets with initial colour
schemes

Plan of staircase

TAVEIRA
SPORTS
ARCHITECTURE

Insets with initial colour
schemes

Cross section

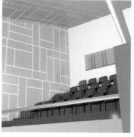
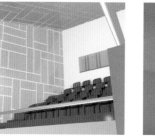

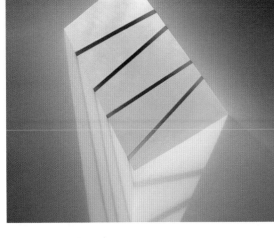

João Lagos Sports Complex

Although tennis has a growing number of players and supporters in Portugal, there is a shortage of top-quality facilities. Oeiras lies on the outskirts of Lisbon and is the home for this new complex, which covers an area of 61,000 square metres. It has been designed to encompass 10 practice courts (3 of which have public benches), a main court, an auxilliary court, changing and equipment-storage facilities and commercial buildings. All courts have clay surfaces.

It is hoped this will become a venue for international tournaments. At present, good transport links are not in place owing to reorganisation of the urban area. The design is a composition of pure volumes that derive from the dimensions and position of the courts. The main court provides covered seating for 10,000 spectators, offers good visibility and has several types of skyboxes. The roof is a metallic structure supported by 8 masts, its lightweight appearance contrasting with the much heavier volumes of the court.

Restaurants, commercial and service areas are a short distance from the main court. The auxilliary court seats 3,500 spectators and also houses a tennis academy. Three levels of underground parking accommodate 3,683 vehicles.

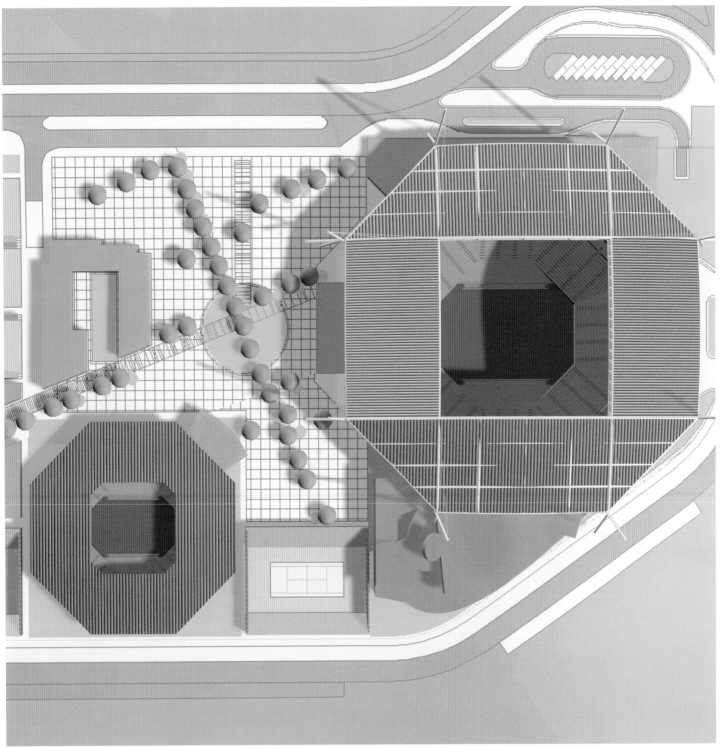

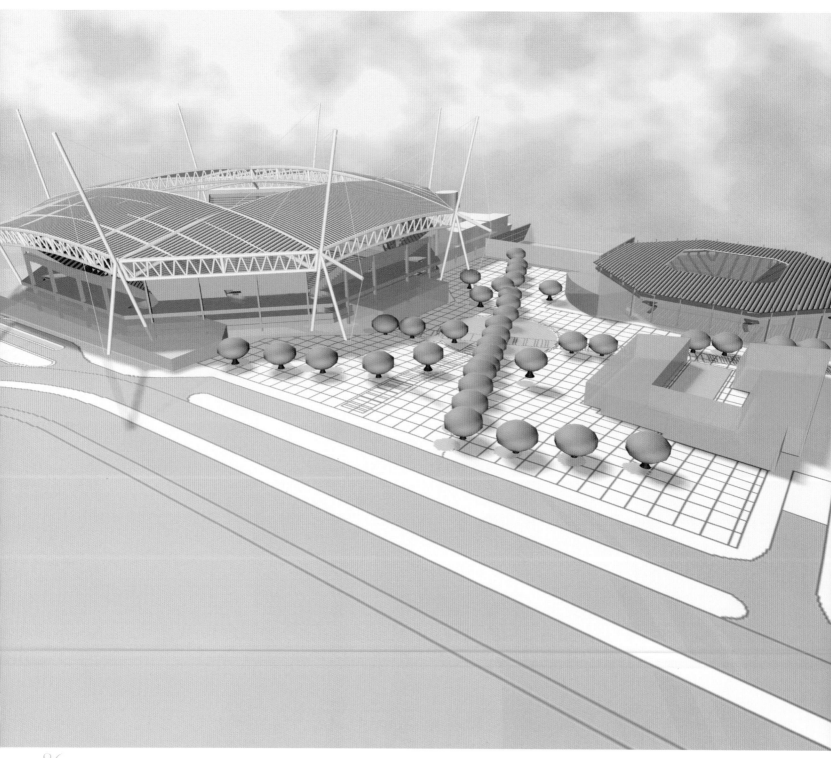

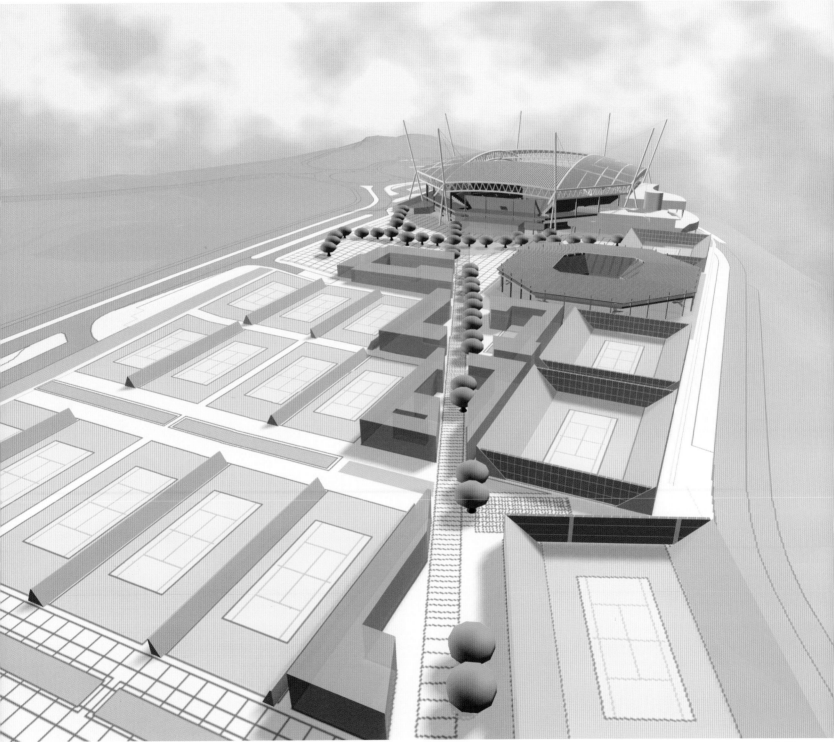

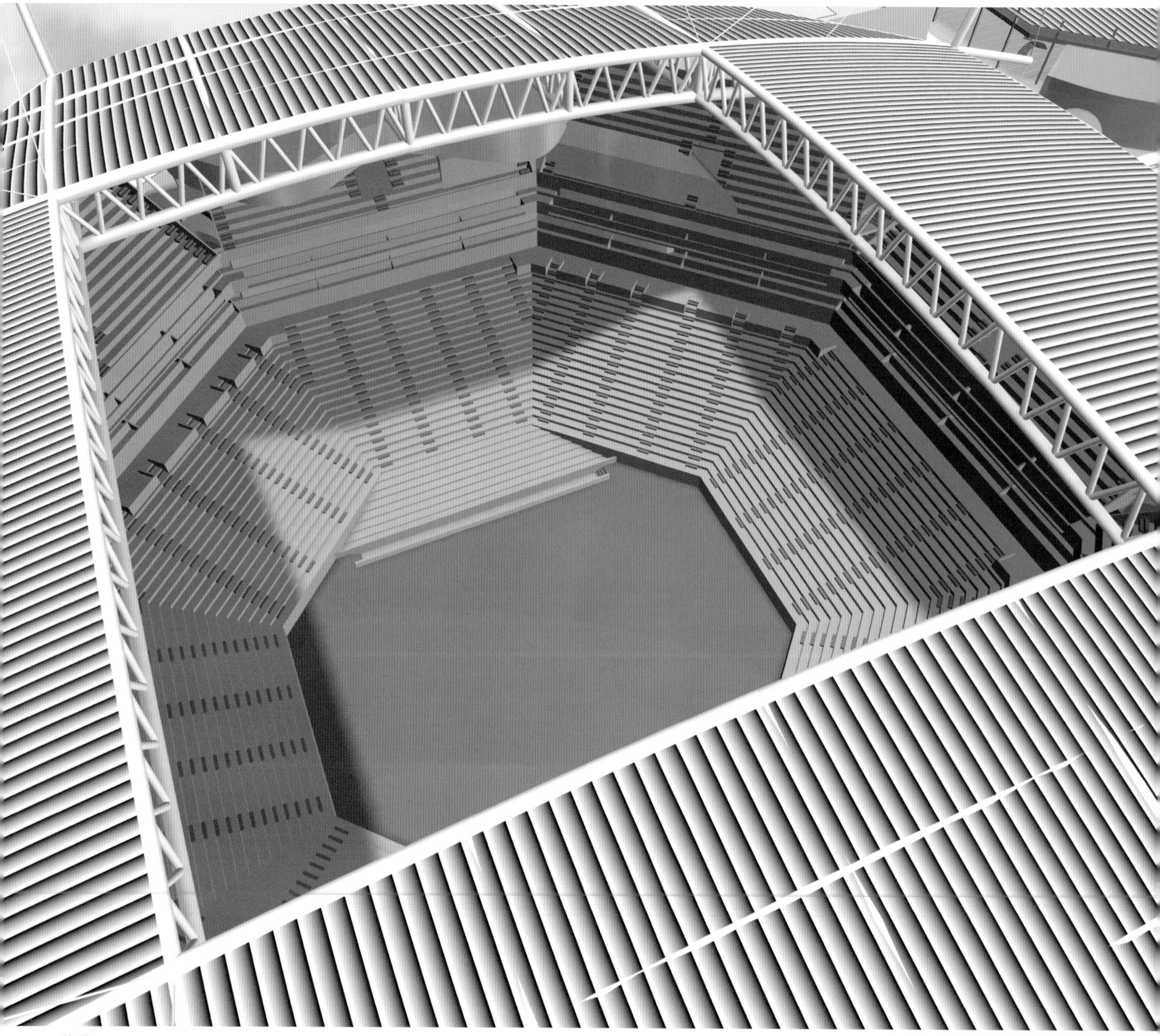

Albufeira Marina Nautical Club

West of Albufeira is the vast plain of Várzea da Orada and it is here that a new tourist and leisure resort, centred around a marina, has been designed by Tomás Taveira. The Nautical Club, currently under construction in the marina, has a site area of 1,184 square metres. Its purpose is to give crew and travellers moored in the marina a convenient meeting place for the duration of their stay.

Jutting out towards the sea like a ship's prow, the strong architecture creates a landmark for incoming boats. The varying levels of the club are presented like decks on a ship; terraces appear as viewing decks while an enclosed area is reminiscent of a ship's bridge. As the Nautical Club is situated at the entrance to the marina, the importance of giving it a welcoming appearance has been a priority. Once safely moored, members can walk to the club via the Miami-style streets surrounding the resort.

At the club, the ground floor will have shops and a seafood restaurant while the first floor has been designed to take advantage of the wonderful panoramic sea views from a restaurant, a bar and the terraces. Disabled members will have access to both floors by using the stair-rail chairlift. It is hoped that the club will provide a convivial 'base' for its transient members, becoming a welcome sight at the end of many a sea journey.

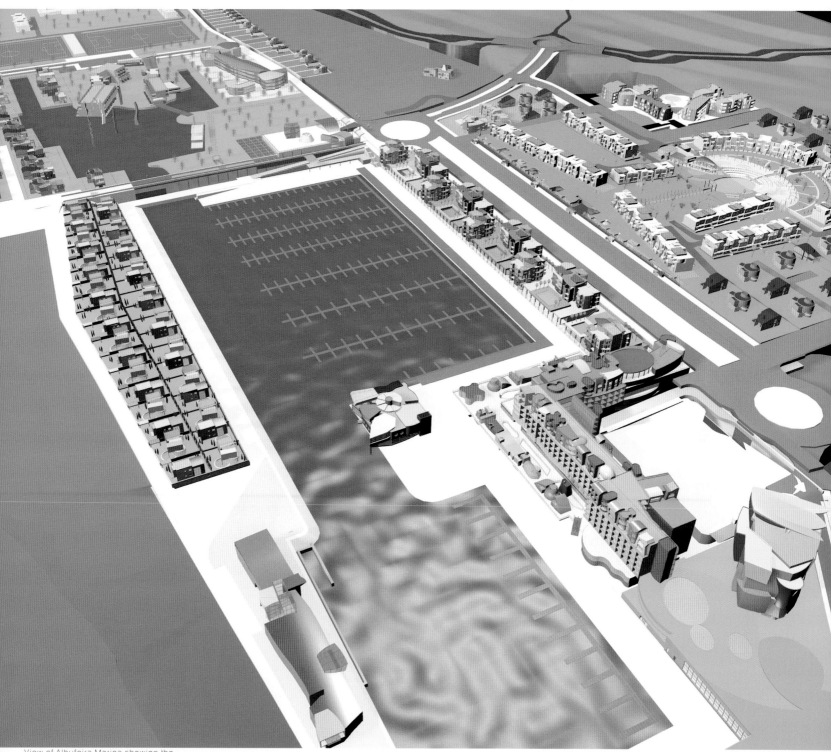

View of Albufeira Marina showing the
Nautical Club in the centre of the marina

Albufeira Marina Nautical Club

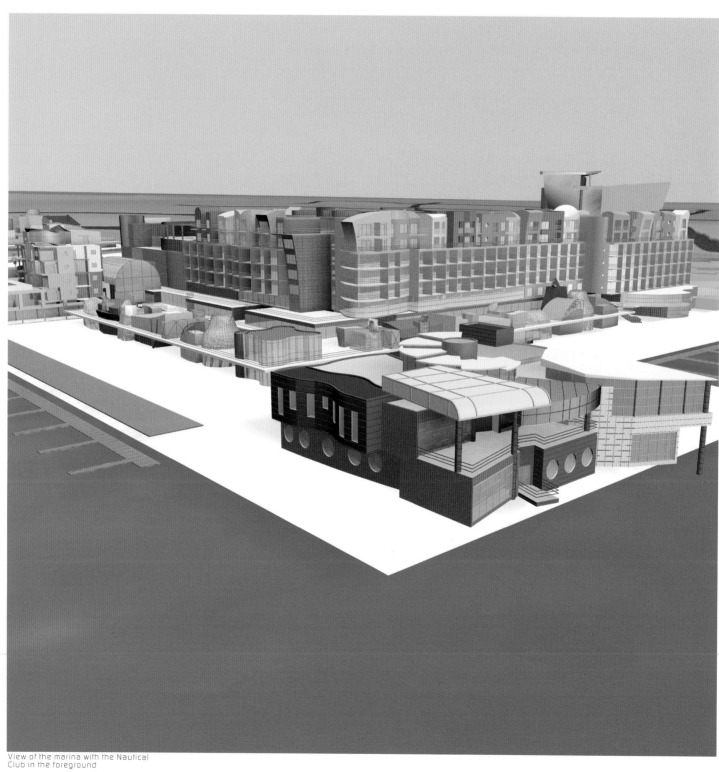

View of the marina with the Nautical
Club in the foreground

View of the Albufeira Marina

Initial design of the main room

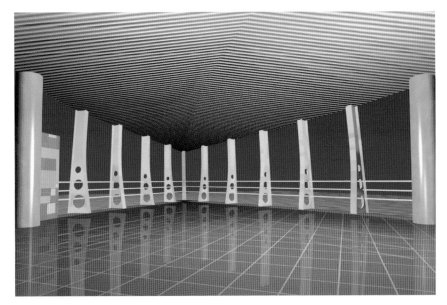

Dr. Magalhães Pessoa Municipal Stadium, Leiria

Lying 130 kilometres north of Lisbon, Leiria is one of the most historic cities in Portugal and home to the country's glass industry. The difference between this and other stadia constructed for the Euro 2004 tournament is that here there is also an athletics track, capable of hosting all official athletics championships. Important issues for the design were: first, the integration of an existing stand and adjustment of the new dimension to the tight space remaining, giving a capacity of 32,000 seats; second, economic limitations imposed by the clubs, municipalities and the government; and third, reducing the stadium capacity to 28,550 after 2004, as one stand will be removed.

The stadium's shape is linked to its insertion into the city. Its curving roof winds round the stadium like the track of a roller coaster, and as the roof dips over the west stand the undulation allows views of the 12th-century castle built in the city centre by the first king of Portugal, instilling a sense of civic pride. Supporting pillars which surround the stadium are linked to the roof by steel beams. Both lighting and sound have been integrated into the inner roof-edge.

Similar in conception and organisation to the Aveiro stadium, the design concentrates on giving a lot of comfort to the spectators. A great deal of thought was given to the layout of the 2 restaurants and 21 bars, to avoid congestion at half-time.

Colour is introduced on the modular precast concrete panels, and their design is very much in keeping with the ideas of the De Stijl architects. The facades are made of alternating coloured panels while walls enclosing access staircases have been constructed from glass bricks, a fitting tribute to the local industry.

The multicoloured seating makes the stadium feel that it is always full and 'alive'. Some indoor parking is available, but the main parking area will be outside the stadium. After 2004 a shopping mall will be introduced to the north of the stadium offering cinemas, shops and restaurants.

Dr. Magalhães Pessoa Municipal Stadium, Leiria

TAVEIRA
SPORTS
ARCHITECTURE

TAVEIRA
SPORTS
ARCHITECTURE

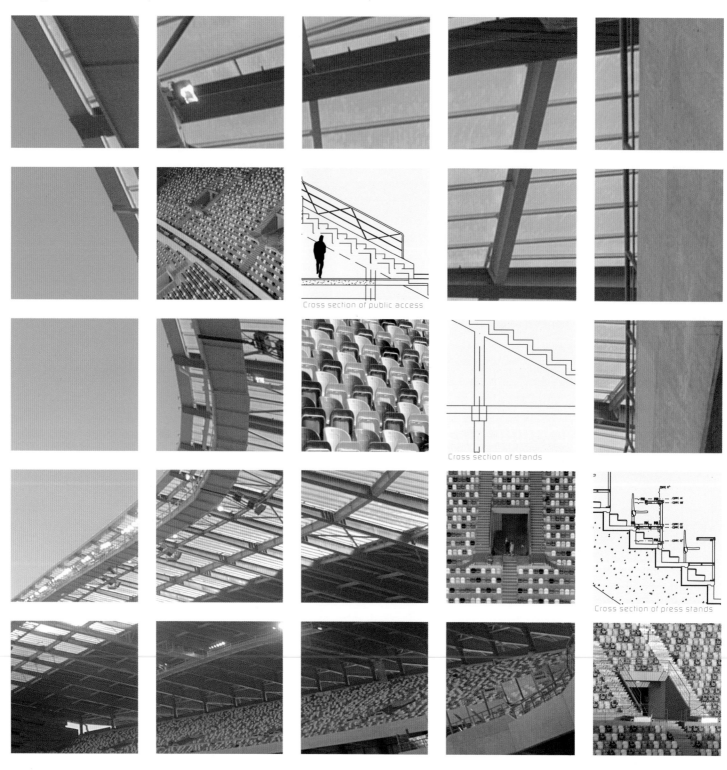

Cross section of public access

Cross section of stands

Cross section of press stands

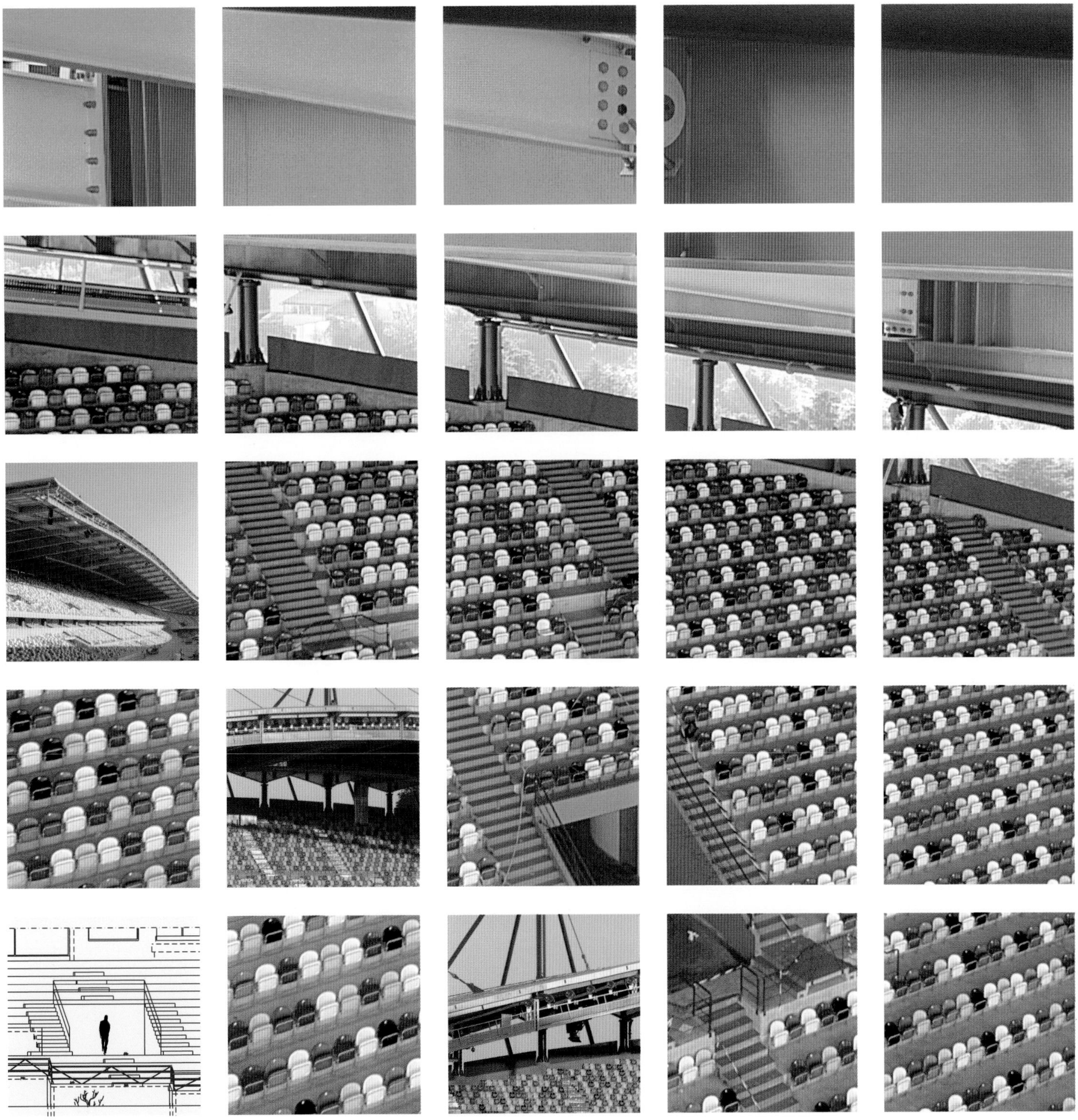

Dr. Magalhães Pessoa Municipal Stadium, Leiria

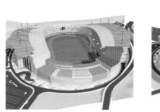  

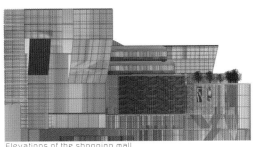

Elevations of the shopping mall

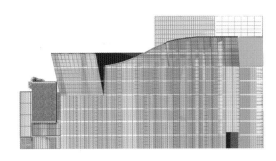

TAVEIRA
SPORTS
ARCHITECTURE

Dr. Magalhães Pessoa Municipal Stadium, Leiria

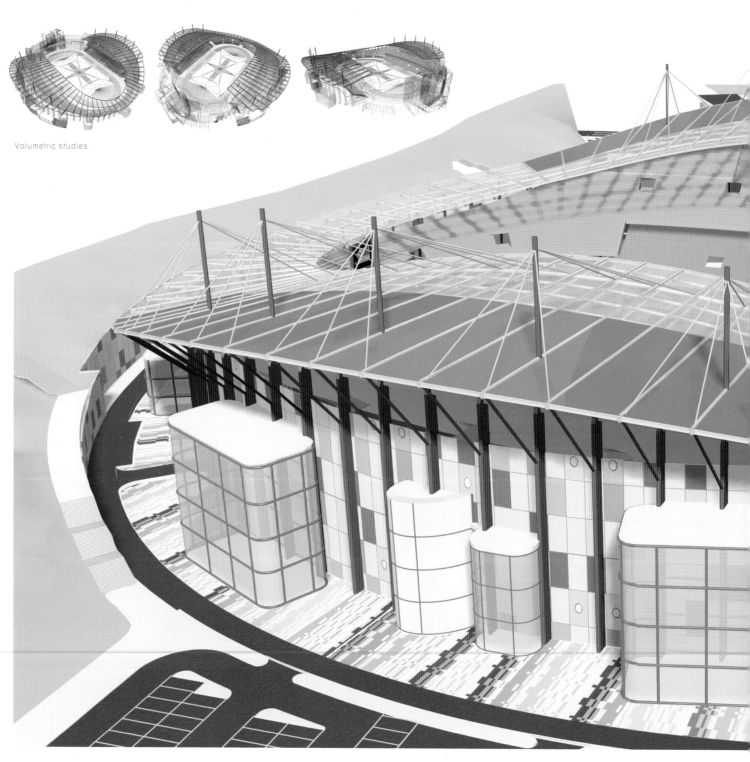

Volumetric studies

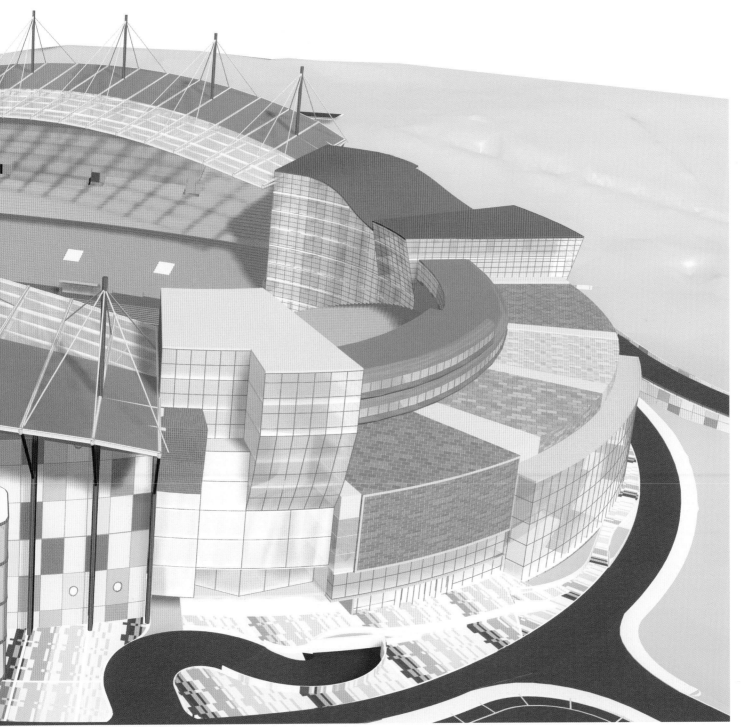

Aveiro Municipal Stadium

Finished in 2003, this completely new stadium is located outside the picturesque city of Aveiro, some 250 kilometres north of Lisbon. It is designed to be a back-up for the Euro 2004 football tournament and therefore complies with all UEFA regulations for stadia used in matches up to the quarter-finals.

Set on top of a hill, in parkland with many mature trees, the site covers some 56,600 square metres. In time the stadium will be incorporated into a long-standing plan for a large sports complex which will house a golf course, tennis courts, swimming pools and a horse-racing track.

Before and after the 2004 tournament, the new stadium will be the home ground for premier league club Beira-Mar. In the future it is also expected to be used as a venue for other events, such as concerts.

Because of lack of space, the base of the stadium forms an imperfect circumference. This gives the stands an attractive sinuous borderline, while the roof, which is suspended above the stands by spiky metal pylons, has the appearance from inside the stadium of an ellipse hovering lightly over the seats.

The stadium resembles as a huge spaceship, an idea further enhanced by its curved precast concrete walls. Each section is coloured, giving the walls the appearance of segments in an orange. The intention behind the colouring is to turn the stadium into an icon in the park. In fact, it is clearly visible from the highway, and thus the stadium becomes a special element in this new urban area.

There are 30,000 seats, 38 exclusively for use by the disabled, and a restricted area for VIPs, managers, referees, physicians, players and journalists. This restricted area is easily distinguished as it uses different forms and materials to the rest of the stadium. Two helicopter pads have also been added.

Concrete, steel and polycarbonate sheets, coloured glass blocks, and metallic structures and plates, have been employed in construction. Ceramic tiles specially designed by the architect Ricardo Taveira have been used on the exterior. Access is controlled by 8 staircases and elevators on the periphery of the stadium. Further facilities include 7,000 outdoor parking places, 12 shops, 34 bars and 2 restaurants.

TAVEIRA
SPORTS
ARCHITECTURE

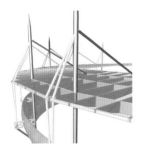

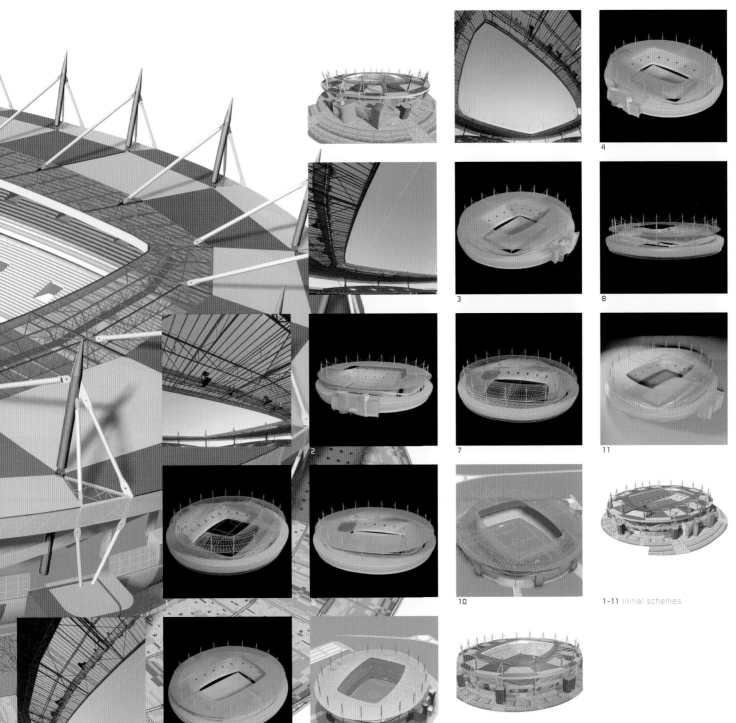

1-11 Initial schemes

Initial designs for the roof

TAVEIRA
SPORTS
ARCHITECTURE

124

125

TAVEIRA
SPORTS
ARCHITECTURE

Plan of the stands

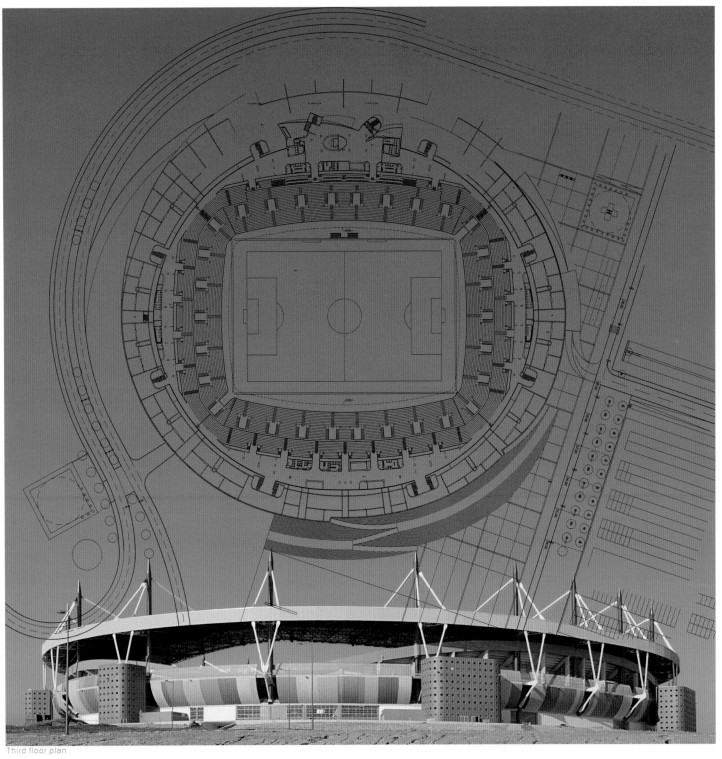

Third floor plan

Aveiro Municipal Stadium

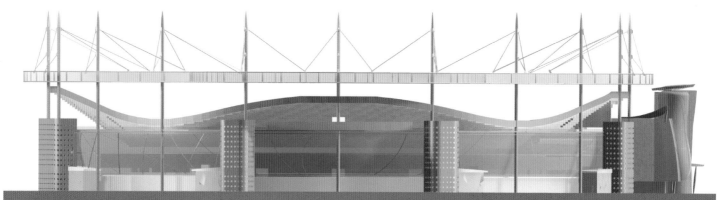

Initial scheme, north elevation

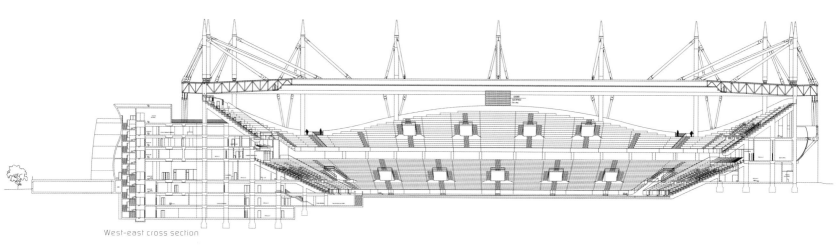

West-east cross section

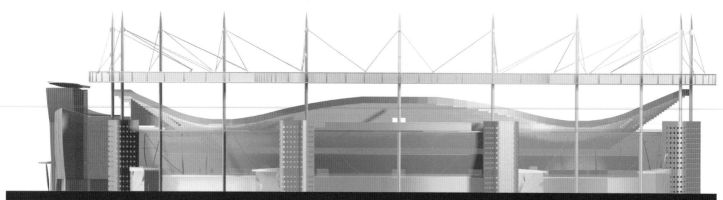

Initial scheme, south elevation

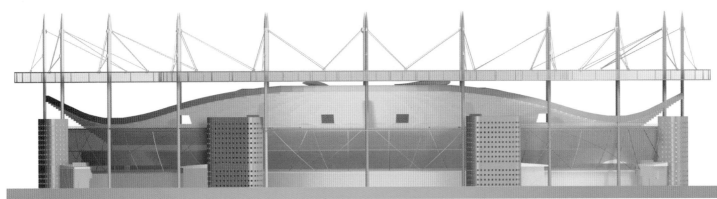

Initial scheme, east elevation

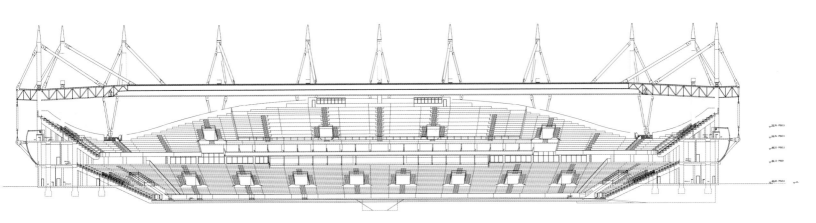

South-north cross section

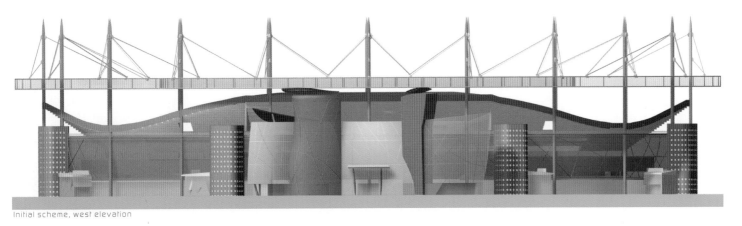

Initial scheme, west elevation

TAVEIRA
SPORTS
ARCHITECTURE

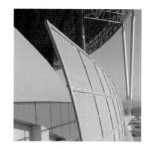

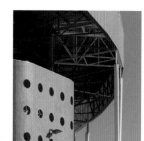

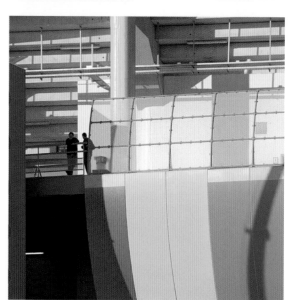

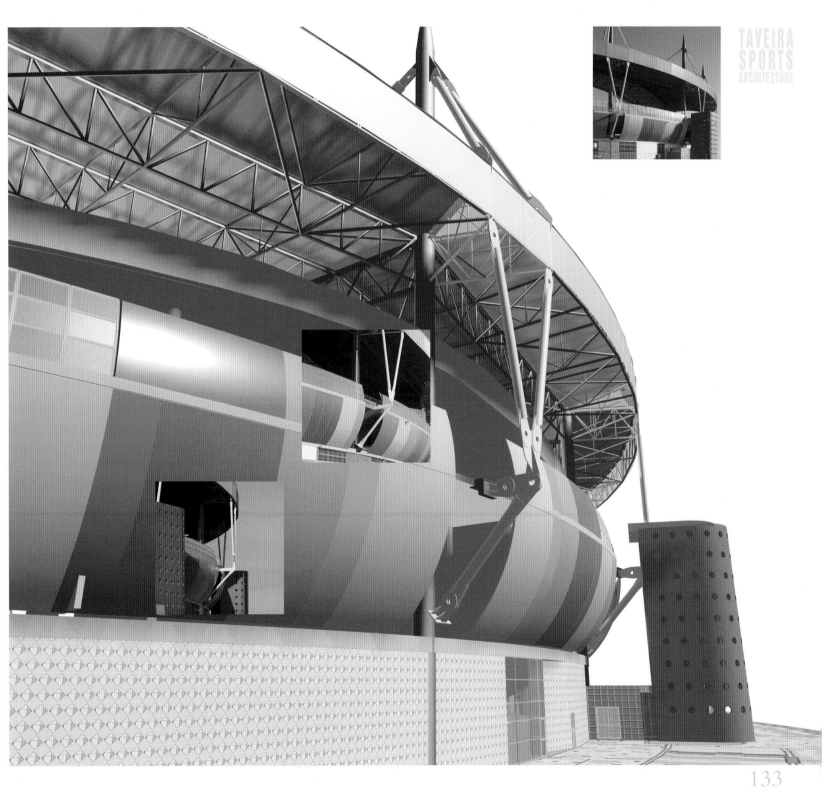

Leões de Porto Salvo Sports Centre

Clube Recreative Leões de Porto Salvo in Porto Salvo, Oeiras, on the outskirts of Lisbon, ran a private competition to design a new sports pavilion. It had to accommodate amateur sporting activities including basketball, volleyball and gymnastics.

The concept was based on pure geometric forms where the oval shape asserts itself as the constructive solution, flanked by a long-lined body that opens the volumes to an intersecting trellis. The simplicity of this concept translates into an optimisation of functionality and a cost-effective structure.

The main building covers 4,500 square metres. Dressing rooms and headquarters are in the long building, which has two links to the pavilion; this allows both buildings to be completely independent. The oval structure has an inclined roof and the roof of the other is curved to assist drainage and give the structures an unusual volume. Each roof is constructed in steel sheets. Glass blocks are used in the building's facade, while the external walls are mostly covered with ceramic tiles creating a graphic composition that is highlighted by the use of colour. The colours, chosen by Tomás Taveira, relate to the different volumes. This uniformity of materials, mainly ceramic, specified, studied patterns and soft architectural shapes create a striking colour note in the local urban landscape.

Although there is no parking on site the surrounding streets offer possibilities. The exterior spaces have been landscaped with grass, interspersed with small amphitheatres and terraces. An exhibition area and a coffee shop are located in the foyer.

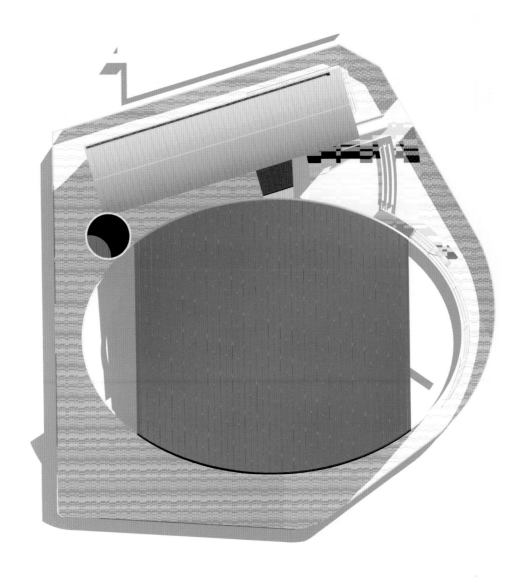

Roof plan

Leões de Porto Salvo Sports Centre

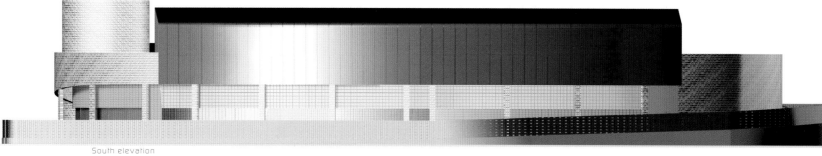

South elevation

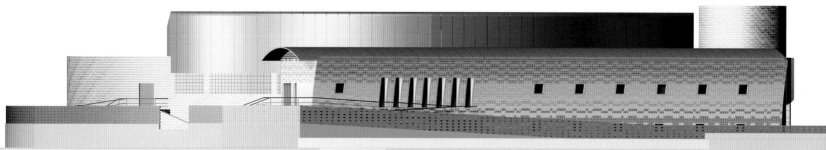

North elevation

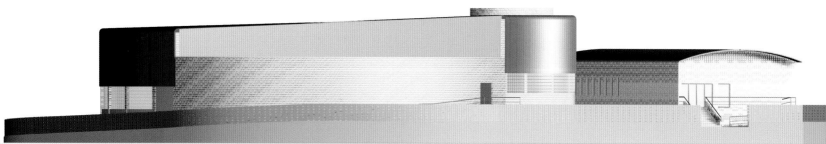

East elevation

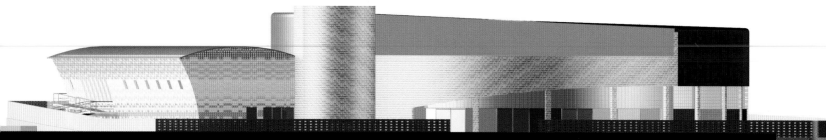

West elevation

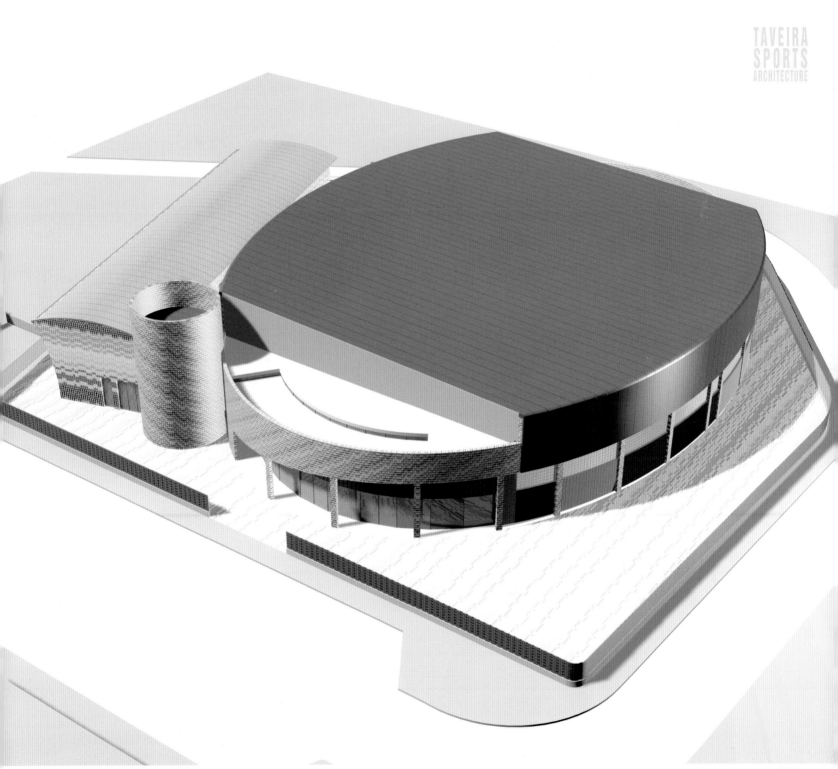

Leões de Porto Salvo Sports Centre

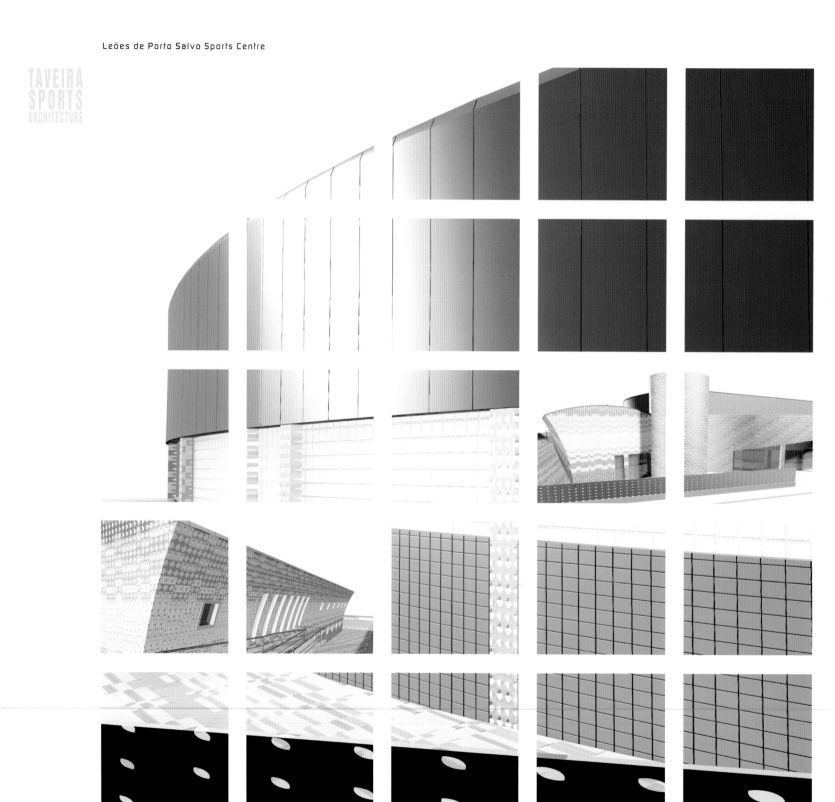

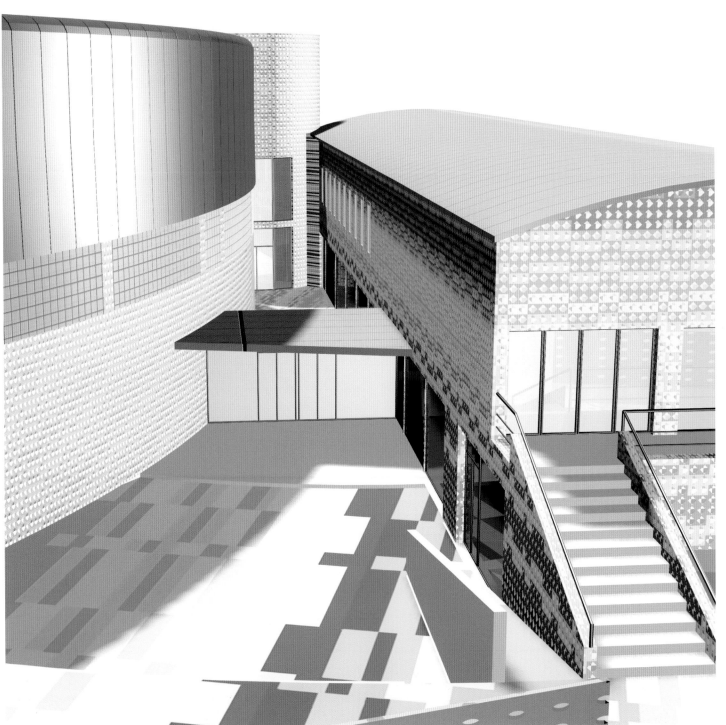

139

Leões de Porto Salvo Sports Centre

TAVEIRA
SPORTS
ARCHITECTURE

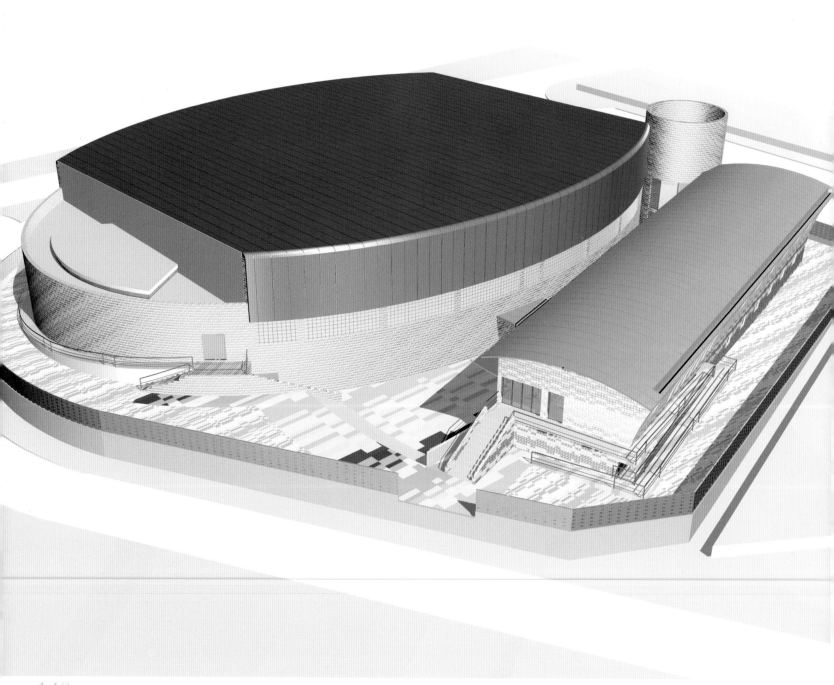

Curriculum Vitae and List of Works

Born
•Born in Lisbon, 22 November 1938.

Education
•1963–68 Fundação Calouste Gulbenkian scholarship. Graduated in architecture from the Escola Superior de Belas Artes de Lisboa. •1977/78 SPURS Program scholarship, Massachusetts Institute of Technology, Boston, USA.

Teaching
•1971 invited to work at ESBAL as an assistant in the subjects of architecture (fifth year) and architecture theory and history (fourth year). Professor of Architecture since February 1974. •Divides activity between his career of urban planning architect and that of researcher in the theory of the urban phenomenon and urban and regional planning, and researcher in the theory of taste based on the architecture theory of design and fashion. •Responsible for the urban and regional planning nucleus of the Architecture Department of ESBAL in 1975, 1976 and 1977. •In 1975 Taveira initiated collaboration at the Universidad Nova de Lisboa on the subject 'Regional Unbalance in a Changing Portugal'. •In 1977 he joined MIT (Massachusetts Institute of Technology) as Fellow of the SPURS Program (special post-graduate programme for urban and regional planning for developing countries). •Tomás Taveira was the creator of the design architecture degree in Portugal, which licensed its first professionals in 1999.

Affiliations
•Member of the Permanent Regional Committee of the International Federation of Urbanism, Housing and Territory Arrangement (FIUHAT), American Institute of Planners (AIP), International Association of Art Critics (AICA – Portuguese Section), International Architects Union (UIA), International Urbanists Union (UIU) and of the National Academy of Fine Arts of Lisbon.•Organised the International Architecture Symposium of Lisbon. Participated together with Charles Moore, Ricardo Bofill and Mario Botta among others, at the NEOCON 18 (International Architecture Congress), Chicago.

Exhibitions
•Architectural works, drawings and objects exhibited in Galerias Cómicos and Amoreiras, Lisbon; Cooperativa Árvore, Oporto; Expositions Room, Casino da Póvoa; Arco 85 and 86, Madrid International Fair; Exhibition of current Iberian architecture in Almagro, Spain. Exhibition of objects in Bordeaux; architecture exhibitions in Barcelona, Rio de Janeiro, São Paulo and Buenos Aires; participation in Art LA 87 in Los Angeles and Habité 88 in France. •1984 Valmor Award and City of Lisbon Municipal Award.

Articles
•1975–76 *Jornal Novo* ('Regional Planning'); Diário de Notícias ('Urban Planning'); Diário de Lisboa ('Theory of Intervention in Society'); and *Expresso* ('Social Housing and Teaching'). Theoretical works published in *Domus*, *Progressive Architecture* and *Arquitectura Portuguesa*, *Revista LUI*, *A+U*, *Emois*

Books
•*Tomás Taveira*, St Martin's Press, New York, 1991.
•*Tomás Taveria*, Architectural Monograph No.37, Academy Editions, London, 1994.
•*Tomás Taveira*, Artmedia Press, London, 2002

Books by Tomás Taveira
•1974 *Discurso da Cidade*; •1976 *Análise Regional do Arquipélago dos Açores*; •1982 *Estudo de Renovação Urbana da Área do Martim Moniz* – José De Figueiredo Award (Academia Nacional De Belas Artes – 1982); •*Regional Growth and Transportation Planning – a case of simultaneous prediction of output, income and transportation demand, using a pocket calculator* TI 58/79 (to be published by the Massachusetts Institute of Technology).

Industrial design
•Coordinator of the design exhibitions for 'Lisboa Capital da Cultura/94'. •Chair 'Laura' produced by Calligharis. •In association with Ricardo Taveira, the ceramic lining of the underground station of Olaias, in Lisbon. •Set of teapots produced by Fábrica de Porcelanas da Batalha. •Sofas 'Fernando Pessoa' for Dimensão. •Sofa 'Gaivota' for Dimensão. •Chairs 'Richy', 'Silvia', 'Marcelo' and 'Monica', exhibited at the Santa Monica Museum (Los Angeles). •Collection of transfigured objects of Portuguese traditional ceramics exhibited in Lisbon by Galeria Cómicos in 1986 and in Los Angeles for the International Fair in 1987. •Desk 'Bárbara', owned by the actress Bárbara Carrera and a piece of furniture, 'Draw', also owned by the same actress. •Garden bench 'Gaivota' produced (in production) by ESCOFET in collaboration with Altamira.

Projects and competitions
'67 Banco Português do Atlântico, Avenida Fontes Pereira de Melo, Lisbon.
'70 Apartment block, Palames, Sesimbra.
Mourisca Building, Lisbon.
Storage buildings, Rua Marquês de Olhão.
'71 Urbanisation and projects for Alto do Dafundo.
'72 Residential building, Avenida da República, Costa da Caparica.
Apartment buildings, Môrro da Luz, Luanda.
Residential and office building, Campo Grande.
Quarter with 700 homes, Porte D'Água, Setúbal.
Directional centre, Amoreiras.
'72 Storage building, Cabo Ruivo.
Village housing project, Colinas D'Arge, Portimão, Algarve.
'73 Building next to Palácio Ana Joaquina, Luanda.
Rua Dr João Couto, office building, Brisa headquarters.
Biker Building, Rua Salvador Correia de Sá, Luanda.
Tower block, Praça dos Lusíadas, Luanda.
220 homes, Môrro dos Belgas, Estrada Corimba, Luanda.
Building, Rua dos Pescadores, Costa da Caparica.
Building opposite the city hall, Luanda.
Lisnave kindergarten.
Clinic (preliminary plan), Lisnave.
Trafaria Football Club headquarters.
Residential building, Avenida Comandante Tenreiro, Costa da Caparica.
Sanimar industrial building, Loures.
Campo de Ourique fire brigade headquarters.
Residential buildings next to the fire brigade, Costa da Caparica.
Building in a quarter of Rua Direita de Luanda, Luanda.
Building opposite the Largo da República, Luanda.
Residential block, Rua Frederico Ulrich, Costa da Caparica.

'73/74 Residential buildings for 10,000 inhabitants, Portimão, Algarve.
'74 Burns clinic, Luanda.
Residential building, Avenida do Oceano, Costa da Caparica.
Residential building, Rua Fernão de Magalhães, Costa da Caparica.
Retail and office building, Avenida da Liberdade.
Tranquilidade Insurance Company, retail and office building, Avenida Do Carlos I.
Cultural civic complex, congress hall, hotel and sports centre, Algarve.
Cabos Ávila office and storage building.
Banco Borges & Irmão, 2ª Circular.
Residential building, Praça Sá Linhares, Costa da Caparica.
Província de Angola Newspaper Building, Luanda.
Grupo Desportivo Municipal de Luanda residence and social office.
Residential building, Lançarote de Freitas, Lagos.
Residential building, Praia D'Ana, Algarve.
Tranquilidade Insurance Company office and shop, Avenida da Índia.
Satélite Building office and shop, Gaveto Av. Duarte Pacheco, Amoreiras.
Vilamoura civic and housing complex, Algarve.
'75 Residential and commercial building, Quinta St António, Costa da Caparica.
Residential building, Azinhaga das Veigas, Marvila.
Competition for 360 homes, 'J' zone, Chelas – GHT.
CAR prefabricated housing.
'76 Group of eight colleges, museum and memorial (under assessment at the MEIC).
Competition for restructuring of Fátima Sanctuary.
Hotel for Macao (Taipei Island).
Hotel and office complex, Praia Grande, Macau.
Housing estate, Alcabideche, Cascais.
'76 700 apartments, Areia Preta, Macao.
Holiday Club, Macao.
'77 Secondary school gymnasium, Benfica.
Fundo Fomento de Habitação housing.
Office and shop building, San Sebastião Pedreira.
Housing complex, Rua do Coelho, Macao.
Encosta das Olaias retail and housing complex.
CHESOL Cooperative 2,000 homes, housing programme, Matarraque, Cascais.
'77/78 Housing project, Av. Óscar Monteiro Torres.
2 office buildings, Av. Óscar Monteiro Torres.
'78 Residential building, Monte Gordo.
Hotel Club, Tróia.
Golf Club, Tróia.
Aldeia do Pescador housing, Tróia.
T01 and T02 retail and residential tower blocks, Tróia.
'78/79 Residential and office building, Avenida João XXI.
'79 Armed Forces social services complex competition, Oeiras.
Macao High School, Porto exterior.
Enlargement of Hotel Altis, Oporto.
600 homes, J zone, Malha de Chelas – GHT.
Congress hall competition, Estoril.
'79/80 196 homes for Lar Scalabitano Cooperative, Santarém.
2 residential camps, Jeddah.
'79 120 homes social housing, Calheta, Madeira.
Cais do Sodré Station (CP).

Travessa da Memória residence and shop, Portugal and Colonies.
Vila Real de Trás-os-Montes City Council trucking station.
'80 Marina, Tróia.
Casino and congress hall, Torralta, Tróia.
N4 housing zone, Tróia.
Porto Exterior Stadium, Macao.
Bairro Tamagnini Barbosa social housing, Macao.
Sporting Club da Régua swimming-pool and support buildings.
Implementation of services in the main building of União de Bancos Portugueses.
Instituto de Acção Social de Macau head office.
'81 Banco do Fomento Nacional head office, Rua Mouzinho da Silveira.
Bonança Insurance Company shop and office building, Av. Fontes Pereira de Melo/Rua Actor Tasso.
'O Meu Mundo' Cooperative social housing, Olaias.
Tranquilidade Seguros – EP, Sines, Portalegre and Sacavém.
Meridien Hotel – Petrogal, Lisbon.
Meridien Hotel – Petrogal, Oporto.
'82 Companhia de Seguros Bonança – EP shop and office building, Av. Fontes Pereira de Melo/Rua Martens Ferrão/Rua Andrade Corvo.
Hotel Altis , Oporto.
Office and commerce building, Av. Norton de Matos, Torres do Tejo.
Areeiro Trucking Central.
Abu Dhabi congress hall.
'83 Marconi head office competition.
Instituto Emissor de Macao.
'84 Míele installation, Carnaxide.
Office building, Av. da República, Lisbon.
Monument to 25 April on the rotunda of Encosta das Olaias.
'85 Praça Marquês do Pombal commercial building, Lisbon.
Centro de Formação Profissional, Faro.
'86 Retail and residential complex including two hotels, Viseu.
'87 Retail and residential building, Calçada do Monte.
Residential building, Rua de Santana à Lapa, Lisbon.
Urban plan, Quinta das Camareiras, Lisbon.
Sta Catarina Cultural Cooperative, Lisbon.
Estoril Tennis Club.
Civic centre for the city of Castelo Branco.
Campo Pequeno Bullfighting Arena, remodelling, including shopping centre and arena services, Lisbon.
Hospital Júlio de Matos site urban plan, including residential, commercial and social services.
'87 Hospital Curry Cabral site urban plan, Lisbon.
'88 D. Pedro Hotel, Amoreiras, Lisbon.
Senhora do Pilar urban plan, including retail and residential, Vila Nova de Gaia.
Hilton Complex, shopping centre and congress hall, Lisbon.
Quartier Rochelongue – Sebli, Cap D'Age, France.
Belém Cultural Centre competition.
Portucel head office competition.
'89 Sea Justice Court building, Hamburg.
Sport Lisbon and Benfica complex,including housing, offices and medical centre.
Cooperativa de S Pedro home and school building for the handicapped, Barcarena.
Azinhal Monographic Museum, Faro.
'90 Housing, shopping centre and hotel, Vila Franca de Xira.
La Défense two office towers, Paris.
Faro City Council historical archive and library.
Alto da Pampilheira medical centre, Cascais.
Trade centre, Bom Jesus, Funchal.
SGS social housing, Freguesia da Camacha, Funchal.
'90 Jardim Suspenso D. Mécia office building.
Madeira Palace apartment block.
'91 Câmara de Lobos apartments and hotel, Madeira.
Hotel, Alverca.
Crédito Predial Português Agency, Benfica.
Crédito Predial Português Agency, Pegões.
Crédito Predial Agency remodelling, Campo Pequeno.
BIC Agency, Marquês do Pombal.
Housing, offices and retail, Arrabalde da Ponte, Leiria.
Casal de Santa Lúzia site plan, Rua D Estefânia, Lisbon
Reiheina Church, Funchal.
'92 Crédito Predial Agency, Trajouce.
Portuguese Parliament remodelling and urban plan.
Casal de Santa Lúzia housing, retail and offices, Lisbon.
Associação de Estudantes do Instituto Superior Técnico housing.
'93 Convento de S. Francisco competition, Santarém.
Alvalade Urban Park – Lisbon City Council competition.
Chelas social housing – Lisbon City Council competition.
Dordrecht penitentiary competition, the Netherlands.
Office and retail building, Praça Duque de Saldanha, Lisbon.
'94 Calvanas Station – Metropolitano de Lisboa, EP.
Parque Expo 98 urban studies of Plan 1/Central Areadetail.
Matosinhos site urban and architecture studies.
'97 Housing and retail building, Rua do Viriato, Lisbon.
Parque Tejo e Trancão – Expo 98 administrative centre.
Edifício Terminal da Avenida da Estação study for a multifunctional building, PP1 – EXPO 98.
Tobis Portuguesa office complex including new studios and remodelling of the laboratory.
Setúbal Prison Facility remodelling.
Sintra Prison Facility remodelling.
'98 Cabinda – Director Plan, Angola.
Benfica Stadium roofing and internal remodelling for Euro 2004.
Quinta do Gualdim urban plans, Santarém.
Cooperativa de Habitação Económica – CRL housing, retail and services, Vale Formoso de Cima, Cooplar.
'99 Cooperativa de Habitação Económica – CRL housing, retail and services, Prior Velho (Loures), Cooplar.
Cooperativa de Habitação Económica – CRL housing, retail and services, Prior Velho, Cooplar.
Braga Hospital competition.
Lamego Hospital competition.
Póvoa/Vila do Conde Hospital competition.
Coimbra Pediatric Hospital competition.
Porto Mother Child competition.
Santos Silva Hospital/Gaia competition.
Beja Hospital competition.

Built projects

'67 14 houses in Balaia, Albufeira, Algarve.
Hotel da Balaia, Albufeira, Algarve.
'68 Block of apartments in Balaia, Algarve.
Record store, Rua Frederico Arouca, Cascais.
Edifício Castil, retail and office building, Rua Castilho, Lisbon.
'69 Valentim de Carvalho record factory, Paço D'Arcos.
Torres de Alfragide, 2 two residential buildings, Alfragide.
Amália Rodrigues' house, Odeceixe.
Tróia Mar restaurant, Tróia.
Expositions Pavilion, Tróia.
Shop at the castle, Lisbon.
'71 Ponte do Adoxe apartments.
Club Hotel, Palames, Sesimbra.
'73 House in Queijas.
'74 Apartment block in Miramar, Oporto.
Retail and office building, Av. F. Pereira de Melo, Lisbon.
'75/78 700 homes, J zone, Chelas – GHT.
'76 Adaptation of a pavilion at the Feira Popular de Lisboa – ISCTE (MEIC), Lisbon.
'76/77 Nightclub 'Charlie's Place', Av. Sacadura Cabral, Lisbon.
'76/77 Junta Nacional dos Produtos Pecuários headquarters building, Rua Castilho, Lisbon.
'77/79 Brisa headquarters building, Azinhaga da Fonte.
Residential building, Campo Grande.
'78/79 Residential and office building, Avenida João XXI (IVA Building), Lisbon.
'79/80 196 homes, Lar Scalabitano Cooperative, Santarém.
'79 Rosa Mar Apartment hotel, Tróia.
Marketplace, Aveiras de Cima.
Banco Totta & Açores building, Av. Miguel Bombarda, Lisbon.
'80 Banco do Fomento Nacional building, interior design and services, Av. Casal Ribeiro, Lisbon.
Housing, office, shopping centre, health club and sports complex, Encostas das Olaias, Lisbon.
Apartment hotel T01, Tróia.
Estúdio Treze cinema, Tróia.
Office building, Amoreiras.
400 homes, Santo André, Sines (GHT).
'81 Office, housing and retail buildings, Amoreiras (old Carris).
Tranquilidade Seguros office and commerce buildings, Av. D. Carlos I, Lisbon.
Residential, office and retail building, Calçada da Palma de Baixo, Lisbon.
'83 Banco Nacional Ultramarino headquarters, Av. 5 de Outubro, Lisbon.
'86 Secondary and preparatory school, Macao.
'91 Crédito Predial Português Agency, Benfica and Pegões.
'92 Crédito Predial Português Agency, Trajouce.
BIC Agency, Marquês do Pombal.
'95 Casa do Rio restaurant refurbishment, Ponte da Arrábida, Porto.
'96 Olaias metro station, Lisbon.
External arrangements of the Electricity Museum, Belém.
'97 Shopping centre, cinemas and housing complex, Fátima.
'98 Family house, Leça do Bailio.

'00/02 GNR (police) quarters in Santa Comba Dão.
Cultural and Social Centre in Barrô, Àgueda.
'00/04 Albufeira Pleasure Harbour Project (Albufeira Marina),
Algarve, all buildings being constructed.
'01/03 Dr. Magalhães Pessoa Municipal Stadium, Leiria.
José Alvalade Stadium for Portugal Sporting Club,
Lisbon.
Aveiro Municipal Stadium, Aveiro.
'01/04 Buildings and services integrated into Malha 5,
Lisbon.
Quinta do Anjo (Palmela Village) project, Palmela.
'02/04 Housing in Parque Expo Intervention Area –
Cooperativa Oriente, allotment 02, quarter 1.13,
Lisbon.
Housing in Parque Expo Intervention Area –
Cooperativa Inoqual, quarter 4.45, Lisbon.
'03 Casa do Futuro (Future House), an architectural and
demotic technologies project.

Urban planning/small scale

'69 Urban plan for Bairro da Cruz Picada, Évora, 1,500
inhabitants.
Urban plan for Alvor.
Urban plan in Loures (20 hectares), with proposal
from the town's Director Plan, 6,000 inhabitants.
Urban plan for Alto do Dafundo, 1,000 inhabitants
(Lisbon).
'70 Urban plan for Santa Iria da Azóia, 6,000 inhabitants.
'72 Urban plan for Cova da Piedade, Almada (opposite
Lisnave).
Urban plan for Quinta do Lazarim, Almada.
Urban plan for Porte de Água in Setúbal, 300 homes.
Urban plan for Lagos.
Urban plan for a ground plot in Costa da Caparica, in
between Quinta de Santo António and the Estrada
Nacional.
Urban plan for Alto da Galiza in S João do Estoril, 800
inhabitants.
'73 Urban plan for Bombeiros, in Costa da Caparica.
Plan for Quinta da Granja, Azinhaga da Fonte, Lisbon.
Urban plan for a plot in Loures (Sanimar).
Urban plan for a plot at Praia da Luz, 900 inhabitants,
Algarve.
Urban plan for a parcel of ground at Praia d'Ana, 600
inhabitants, Algarve.
Urban plan for Campolide.
'73/74 Renovation study for quarters in Luanda, Muceque da
Samba, Praia do Bispo and Môrro de Santa Bárbara.
Urban plan for the ordering units 20, 21, 22,
integrated in the Director Plan of the city of Lisbon.
'74 Urban plan for Centro Sul, Almada.
Urban plan for the zone Terras da Costa, in Costa da
Caparica.
'78 Detail plan for the Zona do Sacapeito, Santarém City
Council.
Detail plan for Bairro do Areias, Montijo City Council.
Urban plan for the Tróia peninsula.
Urban plan for Montijo.
Urban plan for Sarilhos Grandes and Lançada.
Urban plan for Pegões Velhos.
'79 Detail plan for the zone for social housing and
services (Sítio dos Vales).
Detail plan for the industrial zone (Parchal), C. Lagos.
Urban plan for Vila Real de Santo António.
Urban plan for Vila Nova de Cacela.

Urban plan for Castro Marim.
Urban plan for Altura.
Urban plan for Faro.
Urban plan for Ribeira Brava (Madeira).
Urban plan for S Jorge (Madeira).
Urban plan for Faial (Madeira).
Urban plan for Paul do Mar (Madeira).
Urban plan for Prazeres (Madeira).
'80 Urban plan for Bairro Tamagnini Barbosa, Macao.

Urban planning/large-scale

'69 Évora – plan for the city and population enquiry.
Urbanisation of Ponta do Adoxe, Tróia, 12,000
inhabitants (40 hectares).
PP7 – Almada – 15,000 inhabitants (60 hectares).
'72/73 Urban plan for 20,000 inhabitants in Môrro dos
Belgas, Luanda.
'72/73 Remodelling plan of downtown Luanda.
Reordering plan of Baía da Samba, Môrro do Acta and
Estrada da Corimba, Luanda.
Plan for a town of 30,000 inhabitants, Luanda.
Urban plan for Algarve, 40,000 inhabitants.
'73/74 Study of an urban structure, for 30,000 inhabitants in
the metropolitan area of Luanda, Secretaria Provincial
das Obras Públicas.
Urban plan for Costa da Caparica.
Urban plan for Trafaria.
Urban plan for Zonas Velhas, Almada.
'77 Urban plan for Porto Exterior, Macao.
Director plan for the city of Santarém.
'78 Director plan for Montijo.
Preliminary studies for construction areas between S.
João da Talha and Santa Iria da Azóial, Loures City
Council.
Preliminary studies for construction areas between
Camarate, Apelação and Lisbon airport.
Preliminary studies of construction areas between
Odivelas and Pontinha.
'79 Transport plan (Vila Real de Trás-Os-Montes).
'80 Transport plan for Faro.
'03/04 Urban plan and architectural projects for Mondego
Village, Coimbra.
Urban plan and architectural projects for Mata de
Sesimbra, Sesimbra.
Urban plan and architectural project for Quinta da
Valenta, Ílhavo.
Urban plan and architectural projects for Quinta da
Boavista, Ílhavo.

Regional planning

'68 Loures – population enquiry. Automatic data treat-
ment, automatic cartography and urban preliminary
plan.
'72/73 Preliminary urban plan, Loures.
'74 Study for a global policy of regional intervention, for
the province of Angola (commissioned by the
Secretaria Provincial das Obras Públicas).
Intervention model and regional development for the
province of Macao (private entity).
'74/75 Urban study for southern Portugal.
'75 Regional planning study for the Azores archipelago.
'77 Ordering plan for the Santarém council.
'77/78 General urban plan for the Ria de Aveiro territorial
area.
'78 General urban plan for Leiria – Marinha Grande.

General urban plan for S. João da Madeira territorial
area – Vila da Feira – Oliveira de Azemeis.

Urban regeneration studies

'72/73 Articulation study of the current Tivoli cinema theatre
for future evolution of the quarter, Lisbon.
'73 Seafront study, Costa da Caparica.
Study of Av. Comandante Tenreiro, Costa da Caparica.
Study of Praça Sá Linhares, Costa da Caparica.
'73/74 Urban regeneration study of Azinhaga da Fonte.
'74 Urban regeneration study of Rua das Amoreiras.
Study of an upper passage over Av. Duarte Pacheco.
Articulation study of the northern side of Av. João XXI,
with Campo Pequeno.
Study of the east side of Campo Pequeno between Av.
dos Estados Unidos da América and Avenida da
Igreja.
Study of the south side of Praça do Santo
Condestável in Campo de Ourique.
Study of two quarters in Quinta de Santo António in
Costa da Caparica.
'80 First stage of the urban renovation plan of the Martim
Moniz area.
'81 Second stage of the urban renovation plan of the
Martim Moniz area.
'00 Detail plan for the Rua Vasco da Gama, numbers 8 to
14, Portela, Loures.